ANOTHER COUNTRY

ANOTHER COUNTRY

Haiku poetry from Wales

EDITORS

Nigel Jenkins

Ken Jones

Lynne Rees

Gomer

Published in 2011 by Gomer Press,
Llandysul, Ceredigion SA44 4JL.

ISBN 978 1 84851 306 8

A CIP record for this title is available from the British Library

This book is published with the financial support of the
Welsh Books Council.

Printed and bound in Wales at
Gomer Press, Llandysul Ceredigion.

CONTENTS

Introduction

Although haiku have been written in Wales since the 1960s, it is still relatively early days for the haiku in this country. If the form remains much misunderstood, there are indications (of which this present anthology is one) that Wales's serious haiku practitioners, increasing in number from fewer than a dozen at the turn of the century to double that figure ten years later – together with a larger number of 'mainstream' poets and creative writing students with an informed, if occasional, interest in the form – have between them contributed to making literary Wales significantly more hospitable to the haiku and associated forms than it used to be.

The doors of most Welsh journals are no longer automatically closed to the haiku poet, and individual haiku and haibun collections from poets in Wales are multiplying, not all of them, these days, from haiku presses in England and America; the British Haiku Society has reported a significant increase in members from Wales – of readers as well as writers of haiku; and practitioner critics are beginning to lay down the critical foundations for the haiku's further development.

At Denbigh in 2001, for the first (and, so far, only) time, the National Eisteddfod awarded a prize for a collection of '*haicw*', in a competition which attracted twelve entrants and was won by the north Pembrokeshire author Eirwyn George.

Now, as the twenty-first century begins its second decade, would seem to be an appropriate time to take stock, by compiling the first ever Welsh national anthology of haiku poetry. Since the early 1990s, there have been various British haiku anthologies, some containing haiku from Wales, and in 2001 Scotland declared its haiku credentials in Alec Finlay's anthology of short-form poetry, *Atoms of Delight*; to date, there has been no anthology of haiku specifically from England.

Our purpose with this volume has been to take the haiku temperature of Wales, rather than more generally to compile an anthology of haiku 'about' Wales. We have solicited, in the main, work from haiku writers who are Welsh-born, those currently living in Wales, and those who have spent a significant part of their lives in the country but may no longer be resident here – rather than the (sometimes impressive) work of the holidaymaker and occasional visitor. Work has been selected, primarily, for its quality as haiku writing, and secondarily for its Welsh interest.

This anthology is, we believe, as close as it is possible to come to a definitive account of the state of haiku writing in contemporary Wales, not that we can claim to have included work by all of the country's significant haiku writers. Some submitted work too late to be included; others – new writers as well as 'mainstream' writers 'coming out' as haikuists – we learned about beyond the point at which we could have invited them to contribute; and we had, reluctantly, to decline the work of one or two, who seemed on this occasion not to have offered us of their best. The biographical notes at the rear of the book, more detailed than is often the case, convey interesting background information as to who, in or of Wales, are currently engaged in making haiku poetry.

The main focus of the anthology must be, of course, the poems themselves. With this in mind the anthology has been constructed around umbrella themes as opposed to being ordered chronologically or alphabetically by author. This organising principle has allowed us to create a journey through and around the ordinary and extra-ordinary aspects of everyday life, rewarding the reader with links and shifts rather than creating a writers' showcase or a lexicon of haiku topics. Four poets have contributed work in Welsh. Of these, one has asked that his work appear in Welsh only; the others have provided fully realised translations in English.

The poems are followed by an afterword which attempts a short history of the haiku and associated forms in Wales, and discusses certain similarities with and differences between the Welsh and the Japanese traditions.

We thank Gomer Press, and Ceri Wyn Jones in particular, for commissioning this anthology and for the enthusiasm and diligence with which they have pursued its publication, at all stages of the production process. That the country's premier publishing house, rather than a small, specialist press, has taken with such alacrity to this project is itself an indication that the haiku and associated forms have taken promising root in Welsh soil.

NIGEL JENKINS
KEN JONES
LYNNE REES

A note on the haiku
and associated forms

A successful haiku may surely be enjoyed by any reader, even without the benefit of background knowledge, but there's no doubt that, as with any art, some understanding of the haiku's purpose and ways of working will greatly enrich a reader's experience of the form. A few explanatory remarks about this specialized and often misunderstood mode of writing might therefore prove helpful – particularly to new readers. See also the Afterword.

In the west, 'haiku' now signifies almost any three-line poem, witty verse, or pithy aphorism. Such offerings may differ widely in terms of content and style, but they will invariably have one feature in common: five syllables in the first line, seven in the second, and five in the third. Just as some readers tend to mistake everything that rhymes for poetry, so there are those who hold that a 5–7–5 syllable count qualifies any three-line form as a haiku, while ignoring other, more significant definers of the form. To talk in this context of 'syllables' and horizontal lines is in any case misleading. A traditional

Japanese haiku appears on the page, often in association with a painting or drawing, as a single vertical line, albeit divisible into three phrases. The word translated as 'syllable' is *'onji'*, but, strictly, *'onji'* doesn't mean 'syllable', it means 'sound symbol', and these sound symbols are shorter than an English or Welsh syllable. It is generally understood by now that approximately twelve English syllables best duplicate the traditional Japanese seventeen-*onji* haiku. Many haiku poets have come to write haiku – and translate Japanese haiku – in fewer syllables, while others are content to vary their approach, even permitting themselves the occasional indulgence of a syllable or two beyond the holy seventeen. Although some haiku have been translated in a four-line format, and some are written as one- or two-liners, most retain a three-line shape, with the second a little longer than the other two, producing an irregular two-three-two rhythm, without rhyme.

There is, of course, much more to the haiku than mere syllable counts and lineation; in concerning ourselves too much with the haiku's outward form, we risk losing sight of its essence. The poems collected in this book attempt to exploit the full potential of the Japanese cultural tradition. They rely on concrete imagery – simple, clear and direct – to *show* what they have to say, rather than spelling it out. In place of explanation and abstraction there is allusion and understatement, paradox and ambiguity, precision and economy. Amidst the irony and dark humour, and the glimpses of everyday life, nothing is quite what it at first seems. For readers who approach them openly, without any expectations or preconceived ideas, there may be momentary shifts from their customary experience of reality. A haiku is such a little thing – barely the length of a breath. Yet, at its most effective, it is a tiny, coiled spring that can release fleeting but subtle insights into how life is. To release the full flavour, please chew slowly.

The above features are amplified and extended in the haibun which we have inserted among the haiku. Here haiku are blended and juxtaposed with prose to create a unique literary synergy that enriches the reader's experience, adding a tension or levels of meaning that would not be present if they were removed.

Haibun are members of the haiku family still little known in the west. The great classic haibun is that by the seventeenth-century haiku master, Matsuo Bashō, commonly translated as *The Narrow Road to the Deep North*. Although the haibun died out in its native Japan over a hundred years ago, it is now being developed in the west, in a variety of styles, as a promising new literary genre.

Two other haiku-related forms, the tanka and the somonka, appear in this anthology.

The five-line tanka, although regarded as the classic Japanese poetic form, has had less influence on western poetry than the haiku. Traditionally, it too is based on a 5–7–5 *onji* pattern, with an additional two lines of seven *onji* apiece; here again, though, western exponents have often made freer, and briefer, with the syllable count than some traditionalists have found acceptable. Tanka, from about 700 to 1200, was the poetry of the Japanese court, in which the expression of love and desire, in addition to an appreciation of nature, was the main purpose of the form. As poetry became more egalitarian around the fifteenth century, and haiku grew in popularity, the tanka – and the courtly class that had sustained it – went into decline. But, under the influence of the emotional openness of western poetry, it was revived in the later nineteenth century as a medium for love poetry, and has attracted increasing attention both in and outside Japan.

The somonka, possibly the least familiar of the forms mentioned here, is an epistolary love poem consisting of pairs of tanka and written by two authors. The somonka published in this anthology was not written by two authors but imagined, by one author, from two different perspectives.

Age and Youth

Dandelion clock
the child's cheeks balloon
and time takes wing

Noragh Jones

she introduces
her baby to his shadow:
he waves, it waves back

Nigel Jenkins

leaving home
the children's bubbles
in spring wind

Matt Morden

Drawing

Lynne Rees

*18″ by 16″, felt tip pen on coloured paper,
by Ffion Richards, age 4*

There is a red house with orange windows and a pink door. There is a black cat whose feet have slipped off the bottom of the page. There is a tree sprouting flowers, petals pushing against the paper's edge, a lavender sky with a sun and a crescent moon. And floating above the roof of the house, two stick people, holding hands, unwilling to come down to earth and decide whether the sun is about to set, or if the moon will make way for dawn, or whether the cat is trying to escape, or climb into the picture and run towards a door that could be closed, or might be on the point of opening.

all the times
I have been wrong
fresh paint

Stolen by a naughty wind
the child's hat
carries off his world

Eloise Williams

Eighteen today
she goes out wearing pink fairy wings
and clutching a wand

Jan Wigley

Did I drink so much
last night? I ask my father's
face, in the mirror.

Marc Evans

Winter power cut
I look at your face
softened in candlelight

Noragh Jones

the barmaid I once
craved – creased now, like me,
and double chinned

Nigel Jenkins

drifting chimney smoke
becomes an October sky
my hair grows grey

John Rowlands

  summer morning sun
up early pruning roses –
  am I getting old?

Joan E. James

unrolling fresh turf
less years ahead of us
than behind us

Lynne Rees

Alzheimer's [A haiku sequence]

forgetting who I am
        I smell a scentless tulip
spy on spiders
        WeaVING

        O U T every morning
filling my handbag with gravel
        BUSIER than ever

ex-housewife dreaming
        jumping out of
                her fading frame
                        she dusts the stars

    who are they
these people who keep coming
                and think they know me?

        too many strangers
            SPATTERING me with words
            SHITTING in the void

        Hope goes out the WindoW
        At last the walls S L I D E   O P E N
            I'm riding the BIG BLACK MARE

Noragh Jones

Beside the lake again

Jane Whittle

alpine sunset
crimson mountains lift the sky
and fade too quickly

As visiting grandparents we take a back seat. Who are these creatures of our blood and bones, speaking another language and yet so strongly linked to us?

I feel older than usual, climbing three flights of stone steps with difficulty, falling asleep after meals, limping on cobbles. No one minds at all. We are cared for, off and on, by four busy people, each with a separate life to lead, but still interactive and codependent. And our presence alters subtle balances, opens up unspoken tensions. Sometimes we all speak our minds, sometimes we just listen. Mostly things happen in the gaps between our words and hugs. We forgive each others' failings and let small irritations pass.

the ducks float by
brush strokes on the empty page
filling spaces

We have time to stand and stare. They do not. We get up late and read novels, taking longer to recover from celebrations.

When I catch sight of myself in the long mirror, reflected by the cruel light of the lake, I feel suddenly fearful – of shopping in French, of fumbling, of forgetfulness, of the future. Now no longer the person my daughter must remember, I watch her run her complex life with amazement. And her daughter, alternately a sophisticated young woman and a petulant child – how has all this happened? Everyone is fragile sometimes. Taking turns to reassure each other, we re-forge loosened links, are rested and restored to life again before we part.

beyond the water
another country becomes clear
now and then

drifting snow
the old sheepdog
feigns a roll

Pamela Brown

An old woman buys snowdrops –
    listens, sixty years ago,
        to a thrush.

Tony Conran

  walking up the hill
we feel for each other –
    feeling our age

Joan E. James

Old couple arm in arm
visiting the crematorium
to see what it'll be like

Noragh Jones

Too much grief
quietly I oil and sharpen
the old chainsaw

Ken Jones

Towards a Liverpool Poem

Tony Conran

1

Smell affecting *Colour* –
    the Mersey yellow with silence
      in the grey morning.

In the phantasmagoria of the city a chance ray of light suddenly opens to immense distance. Way past the surrealism of signs you finger the braille of stonework and bricks, generations, townships. The trees and the pigeons. The private world each knows in its public gardens. The way wind blows, the way sound carries. The smell and the dirt.

And in Liverpool, above all – the river.

2

Loneliness is in the *Colour* of a poem –

    This afternoon
      of other people's children –
        an old man

      resting his boot
        halfway up railings.

Tenderness is in its *Perspective* and *Chronology* –

> A sapling, he called
>   red squirrels down his arm
>   for nuts –
>
> frail now and empty handed,
>   talking to his knees
>   no one answers.

Slenderness is in its claim to *Honour* –

> An old man jiggles a pram –
>   nine month and eighty-nine year
>   turn tired eyes to the river.

Culture and Society

The Skinner Street Salon

Ken Jones

A winding street near the harbour, its broken gutters splash water on the passers by. In the damp westerlies the door sticks. Push hard. The old shop bell gives a cheerful tinkle. Scents and lotions waft on the warm air.

'Bore da, cariad! Nadolig llawen!'[1]

It is Buddug,[2] with her bouffant display of henna'd hair. Like everyone else here she is a woman of strongly voiced opinions.

Gossip of scissors
the combs parting
sheep from goats

---

1 Good morning, darling! Merry Christmas!
2 Boudicca or Boadicea (still in use).

As I settle myself on the end of the bench Modlen[3] appears from behind a mysterious curtained recess like some houri, bearing a tiny tin tray.

Shortest day balancing
a sherry
on a cinnamon cake

Buddug and Modlen combine repartee, mime and therapy – *and* you get a haircut. A racy mix of Wenglish and kitchen Welsh crackles round the little salon. Under the dryers, ancient ladies sip tea. They are the kind you see on Sunday mornings, in their court shoes, clutching their prayer books as they hasten to chapel, all *twt a thaclus.*[4] Yet the bawdy banter here would make a strong man blush. The few men who do venture into this lair exchange their knowing nods and winks.

Modlen beckons me to her chair and swathes me in the National Flag. Some skilful flirting goes with the haircut. 'Now how would you like it this time, dahlin', with that designer stubble of yours?'

Recalling the beards
she has known
her fingers

I tell them about how my old professor of ethnology would spend his summers in Fenland barbers' shops.

---

3 Magdalene.
4 Neat and tidy; prim and proper.

Measuring the customers' heads, he was. To see if there were any *Cymry Cymraeg*[5] heads still there after all that time.

Buddug responds with a play on my name – Ken, the Gaelic for a head, and hence Cen in the Welsh form. Not for the first time, they get into phrenology. Modlen feels my shorn cranium and speculates as to which bumps where might give some clue to the size and potency of the natural member.

Plaster head of painted numbers
its face
gives nothing away

I entice them away with a titbit about the bend sinister in my Anglesey pedigree.

Modlen whisks away the flag and holds up the mirror for my approval. From Buddug a farewell Christmas kiss – full on the lips. 'And another on St David's day. Twice a year is enough for a married man, *cariad*!'

Worn linoleum
she sweeps away my hair
across the cracks and continents

---

5   Pure Welsh.

a try! a try!
Cymru yes! could swing it yet –
the cats leave the room

Nigel Jenkins

Shadow of the pithead
A cricket, two greyhounds
And a thin man smoking

Peter Finch

i love saturday night
he said   then began
crying into his beer

Chris Torrance

from the pub sways
a choir, tied and suited,
on a cloud of aftershave

Nigel Jenkins

leaving chapel –
below her old skirt
a touch of lace

Pamela Brown

bright sunlight
through birch leaves –
fingers ripple the harp

Pamela Brown

Half-remembered face ahead –
  a sudden shared interest
    in cloud formation

Rick Allden

small country town
the bull's rosette
in the butcher's window

Pamela Brown

Outside the boarded church
Rolled carpet and piled chairs
The stack almost reaches heaven

Peter Finch

Collection

Lynne Rees

Each drawer slides out in silence. First the gradations of white – snow, ivory, pearl – then the browns, greens, shades of fleck, all arranged on sheepskin, named, dated, and geographically placed in a fading scrawl. Clutches of plover, ptarmigan, shrike, and here, a golden eagle's non-identical twins – feather-weights in my hands, no albumen or yolk, just cradles of air with tiny man-made holes. While around the room a weight of books: engraved and coloured plates, breeding times, conception, birth, flight. The histories of lives they never lived.

the room darkens
a scuttle of sparrows
in the eaves

Till evening
   six red chessmen and five white
      wait for old friends.

Tony Conran

Short noonday shadows –
   umpires tightening
      tennis nets.

Tony Conran

mobile in right hand,
she trades sweet nothings
as her left scoops poop

Nigel Jenkins

Paris to Milan train
the baby cries
in every language

Karen Hoy

noh play –
watching the throat
behind the mask

Hilary Tann

Lives of the Poets;
immortalised on the page –
a small squashed insect.

Brian White

Yew-shaded tombstone:
On its faint inscription stands
An empty wineglass

Gillian Drake

Month after month
On the councillor's face
A councillor's mask

Peter Finch

a long meeting
ice cubes in the jug
the first to leave

Matt Morden

community meeting
the priest adds up
his mileage claims

Matt Morden

Still playing with words
an old couple linked
by a lifetime of Scrabble

Noragh Jones

An old crofter's home –
    rubble in yellow birch,
        blue shard of a saucer.

Tony Conran

Stitch and Bitch

Mary B. Valencia

It's nearing Christmas time in south Wales and I snip paper snowflakes at the kitchen table, hoping for real flakes to soon fall like feathers.

'Very good, Susan,' Morwyn says. She clicks her metallic knitting needles and purls at an impressive rate without looking at her green cable hat-in-progress. She pushes back her dark hair and sips the red wine I've poured for her. There's a Faye Dunaway gap between her wine-streaked teeth. Morwyn's come round for our weekly stitch and bitch, a coveted evening of craft making and gossip about the lit students and tutors in our graduate programme.

'It's so relaxing,' I say.

Outside someone yells, 'Sod off!' It vibrates in from the cold street. The final football match has just ended and the shaven-headed hooligans kick cans along the sidewalk.

Morwyn's brought the good wool from the Mumbles shop — silky fine — not like my big brown acrylic ball from Knitter's World for £2.99. Words wind around like her angora wool on the needles, easy and smooth.

red onion sprouts green
in water-filled jam jar
flat's first flora

When the doorbell rings, I straighten up and set my scissors down, expecting Bronwyn.

'Stay there, luv,' Morwyn says. She jumps up, 'I told Owen to stop by.' She calls from the narrow hall, 'I hope you don't mind.'

'Al'right,' Owen says. His voice carries to the kitchen. His feet stomp wet prints on the carpet.

'How about these?' He walks in with two fine bottles of red.

Owen drags a chair away from the table and sits down. His knees bend high and bony and his arms fall gangly while he sits on the low metal frame. He rubs and blows into his red hands.

'Al'right then,' he says. He uncorks the first bottle and fills our glasses to the very brim. I heat him up the left-over pesto pasta and apologize that there isn't more.

'It's alright,' he laughs.

He digs into his trench coat pocket and opens what looks like a Galaxy chocolate bar and shaves sweet-smelling hash into a rolling paper.

At the table I cut Celtic cross snowflakes and tape them to the window that's cloudy wet from condensation. Morwyn blushes and takes big sips of wine. Owen rubs her hand and excuses himself to the loo.

'You don't mind he's here, do you?' Morwyn asks.

I shake my head. 'Of course not.' But I do mind.

The toilet flushes and Owen returns quickly and sits quietly. He looks at me with a downturned smile, then he crosses his eyes. His head falls slowly to the side like he is stretching his neck.

'What are you doing?' I ask.

Owen bends further like he is looking for something on the laminate pine floor but then his eyes roll back and his mouth falls open.

'Oh my God!' Morwyn screams. 'Call an ambulance!' She drops her knitting and cradles Owen's head. She cries and moans and presses his Plasticine face to her chest. It isn't 911 here but 999 and I'm thankful I have Tesco phone credits left.

cigarette smoke
swirls over Shiraz
ashes in found seashell

'I'm fine,' Owen says. He squeezes his eyelids like he has a bad headache. He sits up, flattens his trench coat and taps his shoes on the floor.

'They've already sent the paramedics over,' I say.

'I'm sorted, I'm fine,' he laughs. His lips stick to his gums.

'Your lips are white, like my snowflakes.'

I excuse myself to go to the bathroom. The cold porcelain numbs my thighs while I pee. In the rubbish, poking up under unused toilet tissues, is a plastic packet dusted with what looks like flour.

peeling skin
from red wine lips
to apply Merlot gloss

The doorbell rings, again.

I open the door to two stalky men in green slacks and matching polyester jumpers. Garbage collectors?

'Alright, luv, ambulance here,' the shorter one says.

'The patient's conscious now,' I explain, 'Do you still need to come in?'

'We sure do,' he says. He imitates a John Wayne twang.

'I'm Canadian,' I say, not understanding why at this moment, I insist on distinguishing myself from an American.

'Right, luv,' he says. He grabs my chin like I'm a billy goat.

'Whose 'ouse is it 'en?' his partner asks.

'Mine.'

I follow closely behind to catch their expressions when they swing open the kitchen to knitting needles and paper snowflakes. Owen obliges and they take his vitals in the white ambulance parked up on the front curve. Morwyn lights a cigarette and follows them. I pick up Morwyn's knitting from the floor. Over the sink I tug on the yarn, unwind it, row by row – loops appear and disappear. I unwind all the way, staring out to the cement garden wall. It's just grey with a few cracks, no view, no sky, no garden, just flatness staring back.

Cinio Nadolig[6]
boldly praising Iesu[7]
Menu's in English

Peter Finch

Soccer fans gathering
Their talk has the richness
of cabbage soup

Peter Finch

Ex-miner
cups his hand
against the city wind,
and crouches to smoke.

Sarah Coles

---

6   Christmas dinner

7   Jesus

Daily Life

Freezing wind
the dancing clothes
stiffen into people

Ken Jones

early dark
the cathedral visible
only as windows

Karen Hoy

log fire –
turning in the flames
my watched thoughts

Caroline Gourlay

midwinter
the coldness of
the iron latch

Pamela Brown

fe	him
a	and
fi	me
yn	as
un	one
yn	now
awr	in
yn	the
y	night
nos	
	my
'nghysgod	shadow

John Rowlands

ill in bed –
slow passage of a cloud
across the hill

Caroline Gourlay

Two cups of cold tea
clink together on the nightstand
with each creak of the bed.

Sarah Coles

insomnia –
through the door in my head
another door

Caroline Gourlay

Gwe pry' cop	Cobwebs
yng ngwydr ffenestri craciog	in cracked window glass
mae wyneb anhysbys	an unknown face

Arwyn Evans

Sunrise –
   and empty streets
      stiffen to pigeons' claws.

Tony Conran

nothing to wake me
   after the birds
since you oiled the gate

Jane Whittle

a blackbird's song
repeating mantras
   I forget

Jane Whittle

Stepping Out Again

Jane Whittle

Away at last, I sink with relief into a window seat of the early train, so nearly missed, and watch the landscape changing. Time and place begin to stretch into a journey, a poem. Moving swiftly widdershins, sucked inland towards places I escaped from when I put down roots on Celtic shores twenty years ago, we are rolling east again, to be swallowed by strangers. I am nowhere, poised between expectation and memory, looking out of the window of a fast-moving train.

he ploughs a field
and scatters seagulls
miles inland

Once departures meant exciting opportunities; these days I dread facing the dislocation of urban existence, the speed, the noise and the confusion of too much and too many. A quiet life among trees, hills and sheep where time is marked by seasons rather than Bank Holidays, has dissolved my protective skins. In close-up, fellow passengers sway against a moving background, and chat.

rose bay willow herb
her white hair falling softly
pink angora

When the train stops nobody gets off, or on. The white-painted woodwork of the Victorian station flashes a vacant smile as we accelerate past. I change trains at Birmingham, as far inland as you can go, where I lived once, unwillingly, for several years. Now back yards fly past like beads on a necklace – each little world precious to someone. We speed through corridors of glass and steel, factories, pylons, scrap yards, puddles of oily water. Well-dressed passengers crowd the long platforms – all intent on getting somewhere else, quickly.

> travelling south
> we stop talking to each other
> after Oxford

Southampton lies on the Saxon shore where Cerdic landed and began his people's slow progress westwards across Britain. The old tribes gradually retreated, with their language, songs and stories, into the mountains. I used to stand on the east bank of the river Avon, watch the sun go down and long to follow them. So, why come back? To cross the water, briefly, to another country, I step out again. – *Mind the gap!*

> gathered at the door
> waiting to touch down
> without touching

our house for sale
the trees we planted sparkle
with this morning's rain

Lynne Rees

between flights
I summarize my life
for a stranger

Hilary Tann

calling home –
the colour of mother's voice
before her words

Hilary Tann

yno
o
hyd

ar
y
ffôn
ers
oriau

pry
cop

still there / on the phone for ages / spider

John Rowlands

Waddling along
the woodlouse on my carpet
is going places too

Arwyn Evans

    Glimpse of pale flesh;
last of the potato crop
    lifted from the soil.

Brian White

The Cowshed

Rona Laycock

weary three-year-old
up on the cow's bony back
trying to keep warm.

Yellow milk is sloshing rhythmically into a pail. Warm
air, straw, cow breath are all heavy and humid and redo-
lent with life. And then, a tobacco cough and suppressed
oath of a man weary beyond words, his life spent scratch-
ing and scraping to make a living. He wears holed sweat-
ers and trousers with patched knees, his shirt cuffs are
frayed beyond repair but he lifts his voice in song, shout-
ing loud defiant praises to a Welsh deity.

down in the valley
the heron takes a grey fish
under the dawn sky

Never one for Sunday church or chapel, talking directly
to his God, man to man. He questions the cards dealt to
the hill farmer above the Mawddach. Bitter cold of many
winters has gnarled and bent him and the raw mountain
winds have gnawed at his joints.

the child is fearless
lifted high into the air
to see the whole world

The man tilts his cap and smiles, creasing ramshackle
features.

Pushing my reflection
  this wheelbarrow
    full of rain

Ken Jones

she turns on long legs
away from the bar: not
as beautiful as feared

Nigel Jenkins

not knowing what to do
with his belly button fluff –
I put it back

Karen Hoy

The Pint that Follows

Rhys Owain Williams

And so, story unloaded and beer sunk, he asks me, 'Do you think I've done the right thing?' Pause. Yes, I say, but not because it's what he wants to hear. Because it's true. There really is no point in being unhappy. We sit for a few minutes in comfortable silence. There are difficult weeks ahead, I say, but you'll get through them. And then there'll be something else, something new, and you'll feel better. He smiles, half-believing me. I cringe at how rehearsed my response sounds, as if I've lifted it from a film.

> Frothy dregs drained –
> a glass
> ready to be refilled

We'll be here again, having this pint. Maybe I'll be the one with the reddened eyes and sleep-starved skin. Maybe it'll be him. But regardless of which one of us it is, the other will be here. Buying the pints. Lending his ears.

market stall
buying the smell
of tomatoes

Lynne Rees

crescent moon:
the clink of the bull's ring
along the gate

Pamela Brown

mist in the valley
cows' breath creeps
    from the byre

Pamela Brown

'Worrying the carcase of an old song'[8]

Ken Jones

Lying in wait
the morning of a day
waiting to happen

Down a broad, bracken-filled valley the elderly couple
over from England. Immaculate ramblers. He, map case
dangling from his neck, so sure of where he's going. She,
a little nervous, lags behind.

Treacherously, the red pecked line of the Ordnance Survey
Right of Way snakes off into the bracken. Unaware, they
push on through a broken gate, *DIM SAESON*[9] in a shaky
hand.

In the bleached silence
of a dried-up stream
bones picked clean

Past a shabby little farm, scabby corrugated iron and
knots of orange bailer twine, the track beckons them on.
Arms crossed, he is ready for them.

Smug, is it? Think with their bloody map they know
everything there is to know.

---

8   The title is the last line of a poem by R. S. Thomas, 'Welsh Landscape'.

9   No English

'A very good day to you!'

'You're trespassing, man! Go back the way you came!'

'Now let's be reasonable. According to the map, we're on a right of way, you know.' Red faced, he fumbles with his map.

> Knight of the shire
> his iron visor
> clamped shut

'Don't you go telling me about my land. The path's over there, under the bracken.' Eyes bulging, he waves his stick.

> Taut for war
> his white knuckles
> on the strung bow

Down the road. 'The Old Chapel' now, but 'Capel Seion'[10] it was when father had raised the hwyl.[11] And the school is somebody's holiday home. The shop bought by a couple from the English Midlands. Nice enough they are, but, well … Tea towels and stuffed red dragons. In there, you feel awkward speaking your own language.

She plucks at his sleeve, a careworn woman in a print apron.

---

10   Zion, the Promised Land
11   Religious fervour

'Chware teg, Glyn. Digon yw digon.'[12]

'George, *please* don't! That's enough,' pleads the other woman.

The women exchange glances. George shrugs his shoulders, straightens his back, and brushes past. Glyn, hands on hips, 'sees him off'.

> Bony rocks
> thrust through thin pasture
> the valley reappears

---

12 Fair play, Glyn. Enough is enough.

train to catch
shaving just a leg patch
for ripped jeans

Karen Hoy

Aber's first roundabout
The whole world turns
Differently now

Marc Evans

Another weekend over, under a sky of stars I empty the car.

Jon Summers

mountain home the distant clunk of the cattle grid

Pamela Brown

A neighbour and I
leaning on a field gate
viewing different worlds

Noragh Jones

afternoon fog
the point of the meeting
gets lost in it

Matt Morden

Ageing address book
the living squeezed
between the dead

Ken Jones

Exits and Entrances

all those things
I wish now I'd asked you
snow falling

Caroline Gourlay

at sunset
my shadow
grows absent

Humberto Gatica

on the porch
            her empty rocker
rocked now by the breeze

Nigel Jenkins

In the Air

Lynne Rees

In memory of Lillian Crosse 1921-1998

> sprinkling her ashes
> on the rocks at low tide
> the long walk back

Chairs are stubbornly empty of her – the wooden bench in the garden, the pine carver at the kitchen table, the small upholstered armchair that fitted her exactly, the curve of its sides mirroring the slope of her shoulders as she sat knitting, fingers tugging and twisting a length of wool.

But she's in the air every time I smell smoke from menthol cigarettes that she tried to convince me would only smell of mint, in the whispers of her hand lotion that refuses to run out, the breath of wax in a tube of Rimmel lipstick I've worn to a raspberry stump. And this bar of nameless amber soap I keep beside the kitchen sink, torn between wanting to save it and loving the woody lather flowering in my hands.

> break in the clouds
> a shadow runs
> across the lawn

she moves out
filling the empty room
spring light

Humberto Gatica

Two solitudes to put away
     nakedness, and the bride's
          white hat

Tony Conran

Through the house
slowly
clutching the wind
in empty rooms

Arwyn Evans

so much bright air
between the walls where they lived
and died

Jane Whittle

Bleak day in Morriston
the cemetery grows colder
in the dying sun

Brian White

Chwerthin o gwmpas y beddau
'dyddiau dyn sydd fel glaswelltyn'
ond 'picnic' yw heddiw

Laughter among the graves
'the days of man are as grass'
but today's a picnic

Noragh Jones

White garlic in bloom
　　between gravestones
　　　　the war tents of shrews

Tony Conran

again this year
the wind-sown poppies
flower between stones

Lynne Rees

sharing a grave:
two strangers
　　　　(her husbands)
　　　　waiting for her

Rhys Owain Williams

Paying my respects.
talk is strained
but not the tea

Marc Evans

Old snow waits, ticking
    in the thaw and the
        helplessness of rain

Tony Conran

Gwynt yn y dderwen
A'i grafanc am ddeilen grin
Egni marwolaeth

Eirwyn George

last to come
first to go   the bare ash
combs the wind

Chris Torrance

end of the holiday
a square of pale grass
beneath the tent

Matt Morden

Rusty
     spare parts in a hedge
          the afterlife of a plough

Tony Conran

Sunset –
The withered apple tree
Ripe with finches

Marc Evans

year's end
a flock of starlings
bursts from the palm

Lynne Rees

hill-top graves –
their headstones catching
the last of the light

Nigel Jenkins

another new moon
rises over the mountain
I need not climb

Jane Whittle

spring morning
the day a second swallow lands
beside the first

Jane Whittle

the hunting spider
on the door post – tense
to my key in the lock

Philip Gross

hillside cemetery
all gravestones
face the view

Hilary Tann

Burial Day

Tony Conran

Victor Neep (d. 1979), painter of derelict industrial Gwynedd, lit by the moon; of abstract still-life, portraits of jagged sculpture-like forms; shaper of terror and wit; sculptor of savage birds and warriors from the detritus of machinery and slate.

All the riff-raff of Caernarfon and Waun Fawr, painters and jazz guitarists, poets, spongers for a drink, an eisteddfod *prifardd*,[13] even a solicitor who'd bought some paintings once – we were all at his funeral that clear January day. I threw my clod of cold earth and heard it rattle on the coffin. There was reassurance in the ordinariness of the sound – minimal, but enough to make me almost cry out loud, 'O my man, my man.' We wandered round the graveyard, trying to be near to each other, but at the last minute avoiding contact. Many of us were old acquaintances because we'd loved him, but now we'd probably never see each other again, or be awkward and unsure if we did.

> Under the silver sky
> Ghost of a half-moon –
> A hallmark.

---

13   A chaired or crowned poet

small and slim
she slips through my thoughts
in a cherryblossom blizzard

Chris Torrance

Oh the whorl of her tiny head
and me the cradle
at last

Jan Wigley

newborn
he stretches his legs into
all this space

Lynne Rees

Willy Harry

> I open the window –
> dogs barking in the nights
> of childhood

He and his men, from a child's viewpoint, were giants who bestrode the forests and rickyards of Gower – with spectacular machines at their command that seemed to make the whole planet tremble.

They came once in the depths of a '50s winter to take timber from our wood, with a saw-bench the size of an aircraft carrier, a traction engine, two low-slung Fordson tractors – and a will unthwarted by any blizzard, injury or mechanical hitch. When the steering on one of the Fordsons failed, they simply manhandled, booted and rammed the front wheels until the tractor took the desired route through the Somme-like mud. In the stillness of a Sunday, the trench-scarred woodland seemed to reel from the week's campaign, a strange silence defined by the dune of sawdust built up beneath that jagged disc of steel.

> at home too
>   a buzzard's cry, the soughing of firs
> remind me of home

Another winter's task was thrashing. Reaped and bound into sheaves in late summer, the corn crop would be piled for a few months into ricks the size of an outhouse, until the blustery morning when Willy and crew rumbled into the yard with traction engine, baler and his red-and-yellow thrashing machine. A spanner, a few words, then the drive-wheels would turn and, clacking and whirring, the belts would start to build the pulse. With a string at each knee to prevent vermin from fleeing up their trouser legs, the men piked the rick sheaf by sheaf into the wooden maw of the thrasher, where the grain was shaken free of the straw and the straw relayed to the baling machine. To my brother and me, the mice were Germans plundering the farm's treasure, or pink nests of infidel Injuns. Heroic under the arms of men sweeping wheat through grey skies, we'd stamp on the babies and flick them half crushed to the cats below, or chase the grown ones with pitchforks and pin them, writhing, to the cobbled yard.

How we were hoisted to fame by the legends spun over midday's ham, cider and tea. And how we cringed at bedtime from the day's bloody deeds, both of us wanting, from now on, to take the Indians' part – for the world, it seemed, was crawling with cowboys.

> sunned earth fizzing
> with rumours of barley
> as the rain sinks home

The last time I saw Willy, in the 1970s, he was gusting down High Street like a snatch of old rick. He was sure of it, he told me, sure: steam was going to come again; he was calling back from the yards of Wales all his old engines to power once more the saw-bench and the thrasher. Swansea's shoppers walked wide of the dribbled chin and those spacey, blue, blood-rimmed eyes. Winnowing today's unmemorable chaff from the abundant grain of yesterday, he was back where I remembered him, uprooting forests and turning to a hurricane the autumn sleep of oats and barley. But time was money; he couldn't stop: he'd an engine up in Penllergaer Woods, there was work to be done. Steam, yes, was coming back, back to redeem us from the terrible folly of oil and electric.

I heard of him a year or two later, trammelled in the depths of age's forest, attempting, with pan and spatula, to fry an entire ham.

> last year's leaves –
> a bushy oak rustling
> in icy winds.

Love and Loss

Uplands

Jayne Rafferty

It's colder now. The shadows are longer, but it can't be later than lunchtime. I'm walking faster and I can feel my nose starting to run, my face pointed down into the knifelike wind. It presses its hands to my back and worries me along the narrow pavements, past Brynmill primary. I was right. It's lunchtime and the kids are out. I see red cheeks and tangled hair, and I think of tantrums and Heinz tomato soup with toast after school and the pure-strength joy of running somewhere fast. I don't run much now but sometimes I think I might like to. There's something good in it, but I can't remember what.

> the school cracks open the children
> swoop and dance a celebration

Gwydr Crescent curves lazily, without you noticing, so one minute you're enclosed in rows of neat houses and the next you're plunged into shops and traffic and people, people everywhere. The noise is oddly deafening.

I love Uplands. I love it. I know the faces, I know the pubs and the women who work in the Spar and the skaters on the steps by Barclays. I didn't like moving out. The flat sits on top of the Rajasthan, on the main road, and it looks like a slum. The outer walls are green tinged cream and peeling. My old window on the top floor, still boarded up with the cardboard I taped over it when it broke last year. The doorway is set back in an alcove and the smells of roasting garlic and cumin seep into it. It smells like home and it suddenly seems so unfair that I don't live here any more, even though I wanted to leave at the time. The flat was wonderful. Nothing worked. There were holes in the floor and we had a rat and several mice running around. In the summer, I'd get home from work at midday and run a cold bath. I'd prop open the window with a can of hairspray and just lie there in the freezing water, sweat running down my neck, a can of lager between my knees, listening to the sounds of road-rage floating up on the spicy air.

There's a sound to an Uplands night. Car alarms and drunks and folk bands in the Celtic Pride. And later, the reassuring clash of the security gate being locked and soft voices talking Turkish, coiling up to my window as the restaurant boys said goodnight in the street. It was like a lullaby, the whole thing. I loved the drunks especially. When I couldn't sleep, I'd prop myself on my elbows in bed and stare out at them. I gave some of them names and got worried about them when I hadn't seem them for three nights in a row. It broke my heart to leave them. Uplands was social. We never locked the door. Our flat became a halfway house for all our friends. It was good to lie on the sofa and hear the grating hump of someone crossing the threshold.

> who is it this time?
> rain specks my pillow
> in the middle of the night

I decide that I want to stick around for a bit, so I go into the Tavern and have a pint, drinking it slowly in the window alcove. The Tavern smells a bit like a church hall – that antique mix of old carpet and wood and furniture polish – pure jumble-sale bliss. The schools have let out now, and red and blue uniforms bob past, heads bent together, coats pulled in against the rising bluster. An old woman in a sari leaves the Age Concern opposite, pulling a pram full of what look to be electrical parts. A skater swerves to avoid her, and the wind carries back his muffled curses. She looks suitably shocked. Next to me, a child is carrying on an earnest conversation with a cat. He looks put out when it doesn't answer.

I love Uplands. A big, dirty village full of delicious, crazy people.

two lizards
entangled in a drainpipe
so much in love

Chris Torrance

leaving his place
the heels of man-socks
around my ankles

Karen Hoy

She waits with me
at the crossing – the light
can't change slowly enough

Alan Kellermann

Hay's almost in –
Summer's too short here
for romance

Marion Carlisle

insomnia
the comfort of his breath
down my spine

Karen Hoy

Somonka[14] – Journeys

Leslie McMurtry

28 February

That extra four pound,
was totally worth this sweet
torture, you dozing
on my shoulder. I'll pretend
this is flirting, the warmth is mine.

Ninety percent sure
you don't want me to touch you.
I'll play innocent,
so I can steal a moment
dozing on your shoulder.

31 March

My eyes face forward,
love, but my heart is where your
hand is, dazzling skin.
This bus takes us to the City,
but I could ride forever.

The easiest part
is never to leave you. I'm
not diverging stops,
not a slaughterhouse lamb, work-
bound. I'm in your ear all day.

---

14 See 'A Note on the Forms'

30 April
The babies cry, blank.
Sitting with you is so—oh!
You've changed it with a
salacious whisper. Take me
home right now, never mind the jam.

Your hair smells sweet; I've
been dying. Time, time, never
enough to gaze, to touch.
I want you home right now, it's
my bed. Forget the spare room.

6 May
My eyes are strix *sand-*
paper, my heart a kept bird.
I've missed the coach, sure.
We spend half our time on buses.
Beg me not to leave. Upstage.

My sore arm, your sweet
smell. Well, we missed it. I don't
mind as you draw, your
eyes sleepy. Let's go away,
to the Outer Hebrides.

migrating geese –
her scent finally
gone from my pillow

Stephen Toft

visiting her family
we make love
almost silently

Stephen Toft

Three boxes of vinyls,
a suitcase full of paperbacks;
two lives meet.

Vicky Thomas

Wife's recorded message
he plays and replays
that strange seductive lilt

Ken Jones

you turn, smile
in that particular way
a promise
that if spoken aloud
I would hold you to

Caroline Gourlay

listening to leaves
thinking of the things
I left unsaid

John Rowlands

winter chill –
catching the look
in your eye

Caroline Gourlay

Winter light
inside our bedroom window
the spider's web abandoned

Ken Jones

touching you
as you lie sleeping
the days shorten

Caroline Gourlay

dry wind blows in a
cold dawn:
                someone's
unutterable sadness

Chris Torrance

Morning

Sarah Coles

Morning settles on the garden with the benign, wet smile of a holy idiot, brushing chilly dew onto bare foot-soles, grubbed by the unswept path. It rests soft elbows on the garden fence, tracing cobwebs with a lazy finger. It says that I can take it if I want it. I pretend not to notice and light a cigarette.

Earth-smells of morning
fade amid my exhaled smoke;
morning coughs but smiles.

The garden is greening with rain and all is swollen in the sea-mist – door and gate and eyelid saturated stubborn. It would take a month of sunshine to draw out all the moisture, make them fit again, but it's too late now, it's autumn already.

Glistening fence-posts
suck rain through shared memories
of being a tree

Inside the house, the air too is moistened by the laundry and last night's words, which condense in rivulets against the coldness of the window pane. Your breath sticks folds of greying net onto the glass as it creeps downward, stitch

by stitch. I wonder how long your presence will circulate
the microclimate of the house now that you're gone.

Morning sky opens
in blue and flashing fork-tail.
Last of the swallows

heno
eto

yn
llenwi'r
gofod
rhyngom

again/ this evening/
filling the space between us/
the scent of honeysuckle

sawr
gwyddfid

John Rowlands

Night breeze
stirs a tree: the sound
of an unshared bed

Alan Kellermann

facing you
I avoid your eyes but
reach out my hand
as if offering you something
you might need one day

Caroline Gourlay

a bullfinch sparks off
into the gloom   an old
sadness returns

Chris Torrance

Bad day
ducks shelter
beneath the hearse

Ken Jones

One Minute Silence
birdsong
and some deeper grief

Ken Jones

Rain and the ghosts of rain
conjure the mountain.
Everything will disappear.

Tony Curtis

A Life Turned to Stone

Noragh Jones

She can't bear to clear out his things after he's gone. She can't bear to have them around her either.

> In the fossil house
> empty clothes, buried words
> a life turned to stone

Everybody says she should leave it all and get away for a while. She decides to be sensible and follow their advice. She has a holiday (if you could call it that) in a quiet hotel by Lake Ullswater. She takes long walks alone on the fells. But these are paths they had walked together for more than twenty summers.

> Following alien boot prints
> only hearing what you said
> after you have gone

Back home she starts sorting out his books and files, his tapes and CDs. Sorting has always soothed her, ever since she was a little girl and her mother passed on her domestic mania for sorting drawers and tidying cupboards. But this sorting is different. This is clearing all traces of hum from the world they created together. This is exorcising his ghost, but she needs his ghost to hang about and go on talking to her.

> Lost lover
> finding their chess board
> endgame unfinished

Sitting at the computer one afternoon she tries to stem the flow of emails still coming in for him. How do you stop people writing to the dead?

> Unanswered messages
> forever orbiting
> planet earth

Eating supper in front of the telly, she watches *Eastenders* and envies the easy drama of made-up lives. Nothing to do, and another long evening stretching ahead. Switching off the telly she faces the unnerving silence. It creeps closer. The air feels too heavy to breathe. She goes to bed at nine and passes the night in the company of the BBC World Service.

> Lying awake
> listening for the board that used to creak
> on his way to the loo

Living Things

Lynne Rees

The weeping willow, despite its name, its curtain of low-sweeping boughs, does not weep over what is lost, does not grieve.

> after her death
> watching the rain
> meeting the river

Beneath the bark, a layer of living cells divides and multiplies, expanding sapwood and heartwood, stretching the bark until it cracks and sheds to fit the new girth.

> laughter lines –
> the scar around my breast
> faded now

Growth: out into the world, down into the dark earth, and up into the light.

Memory and Imagination

no one about yet
except me and a rat
who knows I'm trouble

Nigel Jenkins

starlings
fill the sky
they object to everything

Viv Kelly

Flight of geese
open the sky for dreaming —
that sound

Marion Carlisle

there is something
of my childhood
in the mosquito buzz

Humberto Gatica

Little Brother

Lynne Rees

I

My brother is five years old again. 'Do you want to go on an adventure?' I ask him. I have money in a plastic envelope, bags of sweets, our thick coats. He looks out of the window and says, 'But things are going to get worse.' He's right. The moon shivers across the dark sea as we look out at the lines of rising surf, our hands pressed to the glass. When the storm comes I feel it pound against the chalet's thin wooden walls, through the veil of my dream.

a little boy stares
at his fists full of sand
sails on the horizon

II

My brother is 44 this year and has children by three different women: a daughter of eighteen who has lived in the States for the past twelve years, a boy of eleven whose mother disappeared with him when he was only a few months old, and Morgan, his baby son with Manuela. The invitation to their wedding arrived this week.

warm wind
a man lifts his hands
from the handlebars

My five-year-old brother learnt to play cards in a caravan on a rainy afternoon in North Wales. When he dropped a card and crawled under the table to fetch it my sister and I swapped the remaining ones for four Jacks to give him the game. A grin began to spread across his face as he picked up one card at a time. When he finally realised we'd set him up, he looked at us and said, 'You scrumptious girls.'

crowded promenade
a little boy jumps
the long shadows

Aberafan Beach – Summer of '63

Lynne Rees

We were the first people at our end of Chrome Avenue to have a fridge. Preparation for it had started weeks before – the brick pantry in the corner of the kitchen knocked down, new lino laid on the floor. When it was delivered, neighbours came out to watch its white bulk being trolleyed through the back gate. The next day my mother made ice-lollies from orange squash and I sucked mine until my gums ached.

I was making sandcastles on the beach when I told my friend Kathryn about our new fridge and she hit me over the head with a long-handled spade and ran home crying. My mother said Kathryn didn't like me being different from her. And we were different now. Our butter was hard. We had frozen peas.

> new neighbour:
> secretly inspecting
> her washing-line

The Van-men of Sandfields Estate

after Paul Conneally's 'Around The Rhubarb'

Lynne Rees

They have disappeared now, the van-men of my child-hood. They came to us, street by street with ice-cream, chips, milk and bread. The weight of a silver half-crown piece in my hand. The smell of a fresh sandwich loaf, and my mother cutting off the crust with a silver knife. The bright yellow butter. The summers' heat.

sunlit garden
when did my father grow
an old man's neck?

in the herb garden
bruising memory
between our fingers

Philip Gross

Bloom on wild plums
our mouths
fill with the sound of it

Arwyn Evans

listen!
skins of wild damsons
darkening in the rain

Caroline Gourlay

pungent apple bowl
memories of scorching
summer sex

Eloise Williams

the cracked lintel:
the soundless
        passing of time

Chris Torrance

Shrouded Hills

Arwyn Evans

> Red rock stair –
> the whisper of a falling stream

Water, cutting through the plateau's rim, just as it shows. But the map gives no name.

'Let's call it Ceunant Goch,' he said, 'Red Gulch.'

That was over forty years ago. Today, on my own, the cloud is just above me as I head north across the plateau. Dark pools. Bleached stone scattered wide. 'A herd of woolly mammoths,' he had said.

At the northern rim, a view down Cwm Oergwm – the Bitter Valley. Low cloud clings, curls down its dripping crags. 'Imagine standing here when there's a north wind blowing.'

I reach the point of Fan Big. Far below, the Roman Road passes through The Gap, though I see no part of it. Standing on rock, my toes are on the edge of nothingness

> The smell of mist –
> a raven, nowhere, croaking

I take the steep path down and now, below the cloud, I see The Gap. Head for it. Arrive. And stand.

A day exactly like this, it was, I stood here with my father as he spun his tale: The Legion Lost. I shudder at the shock of ambush. The shower of memories from the hanging mist. The avalanche of . . .

I walk back south, overlooking Neuadd Reservoir. The low light drawn from lake water.

> A thrush begins to sing.
> My father's gentle breathing.

Dreams Wander On

Ken Jones

Window filled with drifting cloud
Earth turns
the day hangs in the air

On the patterned tablecloth the patterned map. A wild, rolling upland, reinforced with sellotape along the folds. The scarcely inhabited parishes of Llanddewi Abergwesyn and Llanfihangel Abergwesyn – I roll them round my mouth. My boots replaced with a magnifying glass and my imagination freed by confinement, I can cross both parishes between sips of coffee.

With a forefinger several hundred yards wide I push my way through dense green rectangles of sitka spruce. I follow my past along the pecked red lines of paths and bridleways, pausing at reminders in fading biro: arrows, crosses, ticks, question and exclamation marks.

Old age enjoyed
'be-wilder-ment'
that tangled, wild-eyed word

A landscape rich only in place names, spread everywhere across the wriggling orange contours. Placeless place names, useful only to the long dead locals. The familiar Welsh of hill and pasture, stream and woodland, repeated over and over again. But now and again my wandering eyeglass pauses. *Tŷ Harlot* – some bucolic brothel? And *Tŷ Sais* – the Englishman's House.

> Broken ribbed house
> its staring windows
> in the western light

Here's Moelprysgau, where I've passed many a haunted night. A sour, boggy place. Its broken fences wander aimlessly through the yellow grass, before losing themselves in blanket spruce. At least four recorded murders hereabouts, three by Evan Edwards. Stabbed his pregnant wife near Pen Bwlch Rhyd y Meirch. She'd discovered he was keeping a mistress down at Pontrhydfendigaid – 'The-Bridge-at-the-Ford-of-the-Blessed-Virgin'.

> Rising wind
> the moonlit pines
> mutter and screech

And yet … the great Revivals … those singing bands of men and women striding with their lanterns across my map. 'Guide us O thou great Jehovah through our life's tempestuous sea.'

This map once framed 'an original race … who had cultivated their own individuality from generation to generation without let or hindrance, and where every man, woman and child was an entirely new edition of humanity.'[15]

> Remains of the day
> all the potholes
> filled with silver

---

15   From Ruth Bidgood's *Parishes of the Buzzard* (Goldleaf, 2000), p.197. Ken Jones is grateful to her for the background material used in this haibun.

Nature Observed

open moor a low wind loosens a lark's nest

Pamela Brown

hounded from the parish
by an opera of songbirds
  – scruffy tom

Chris Torrance

Kestrel kills in the pansies
  ignoring
        this most civilised of patios

Tony Conran

unmarked road
the dead mink
holds its shape
Pamela Brown

uncertain sky
the dark centre
of the ram's eye
Pamela Brown

Cysgodion dail yn disgyn   Leaf shadows fall
i'r pwll disglair   into the glistening pond
... gwrandawaf   ... I listen

Arwyn Evans

Two High Backed Chairs

*Any resemblance to any specific person
is wholly coincidental.*

Ken Jones

By firelight
The Lives of the Saints
bound in leather

In our black robes we have filed back from Evensong across the cathedral close. 'You should come more often,' says the canon, who welcomes our Zen retreat in the Deanery. I leave the candlelit meditation hall to prepare for interviews here in the library. Pale evening light filters through the tall Georgian windows, and the sandalwood incense wafts a different odour of sanctity. On a side table the Goddess of Compassion raises her hand in blessing above a box of Kleenex tissues.

Wind scoured beach
to every tiny pebble
its tail of sand

Jack

Young and earnest, all in black, he pads in, sporting a martial arts t-shirt. His designer stubble is well maintained and he takes us both very seriously. I try him with a few playful sallies, but he hangs on to his shoplifted goods. A nice lad in a Zen mask, taken in for further questioning.

> In its little cage
> a clockwork bird
> wound up

Jane

Halting steps, a timid knock, a growl of welcome. Thin and anxious, her clothes dowdy, her hair lank. Life frightens her. But she is brave enough to come here. She and I, we take a kindly interest in her fear. She loves William Blake. 'Joy and woe are woven fine'. A wan smile lights up her face; she will be alright.

> How is it, spider,
> fleeing across
> the bright colours?

David

The stride of a well-established self. He has a degree in Buddhism and goes on about Zen. His Japanese pronunciation is impressive. I stare at his highly polished shoes and wait until he's finished. We shall have to turn out his pockets, to discover where he keeps his anger, his fear, and, hopefully, his love. I discover he is having difficulties at home, so we start there.

Climbing steeply
through storm clouds
fly on the window

Amy

Red salopettes and long blond hair. The way she moves,
she knows a thing or two. She also knows that I know
she's just called in to share the cosmic joke, or something
of that sort. Playfully, I try to test her sense of humour to
destruction, but we end up laughing again.

My false teeth mug
filled to overflowing
with her yellow flowers

Martha

Sensibly dressed and impaled on virtue. She has so much
to do. Peace and justice. Children and aged parents. A
husband, too. And enlightenment on top of all that.
I invite her to reflect on the fact that *Nothing matters;
everything matters* – which is also giving her a hard time.
However, she has taken up singing. There *is* a singing
woman deep inside. But still, as yet…

Round and round
the squirrel woman
in the wheel she's made

Martha's the last one for tonight. In the silence the cathedral clock gathers its strength and strikes ten times, each stroke a little less than perfect. Tears spring in my eyes.

Where sweet water
meets the rising tide
a tang of salt

Oystercatchers huddle
at the river mouth;
    the rumble of thunder.

Brian White

Gan siglo hen ddail   Shaking old leaves
mae'r frân   the crow
yn clwydo mewn lleuad isel   perches in a low moon

Arwyn Evans

frosty bark
    as I squint the Pleiades
of fox, *cadno*, fox, fox[16]

Nigel Jenkins

---

16   *Cadno:* Welsh for 'fox'.

mountain wind
the stillness of a lamb
gathers the crows

Matt Morden

noonday heat
the pony holds a mouthful
of mountain stream

Pamela Brown

mountain stillness –
the loon call
held by the lake

Hilary Tann

a little egret
caught in meditation
and his reflection

Rona Laycock

Pyst o oleuni
Yn dal yr haul yn y nef
Bydd glaw yn gwreichioni

Eirwyn George

Tangle of midges
tempts a silver thrash
to break the surface.
The moon judders.

Stephen White

Summer afternoon –
one clap of thunder
surrounding silence

Arwyn Evans

Air
the feathering
of falcon's breath

Arwyn Evans

on this ancient crab
leafless, sun-facing
a single, yellow fruit

Chris Torrance

The Dying

Ken Jones

Each morning
if the sun shows up
together we climb the hill

For now the turning world is squeezing the sunshine out
of the deep valley of the Rheidol. So each morning I have
to climb higher and higher behind the house to reach
my bright, warm-hearted companion. There I find her
just peeping through the saw-edged line of spruce which
fringes the skyline on the other side of the cwm.

Twilight in Coed Simdde Lwyd – Grey Chimney
Wood – now haunted by the yellow fronds of dying
bracken, standing spectral in the stillness of the evening.
The bracken, the silent oaks, and this old man, all
bewitched together.

Cutting through my reverie
the sharp splatter of rain
on dead leaves

People in the Landscape

A dogfox
   sensing us, pulls
     the sunrise tighter

Tony Conran

The valley   white
with hawthorn trees
I breathe   I breathe

Arwyn Evans

Pilgrimage to Pennant Melangell

Noragh Jones

It's a drizzly May morning when I leave home on the three day walk to Melangell's shrine. My way climbs steeply out of our valley on old miners' tracks, and skirts round Pumlumon, the bare mountain that gives birth to three rivers – the Wye, the Severn and the Rheidol.

I trudge the sheep-grazed moor hour after hour, without sight or sound of human habitation. Is this what pilgrimage is about? Not filling but emptying?

Cerdded trwy'r dydd	Walking the whole day through
heb gwrdd â neb	meeting no one
dim ond fi fy hun	but myself

Noon in the stone ruins of Bugeilyn. I eat damp sandwiches, crouching in a windowless window, half in and half out of the rain. Then I get up speed walking a landrover track to Glaslyn, the blue green lake that's misted in grey drizzle. The rain finally drifts off to the east, and with it goes the emptiness I'm getting used to.

Torri'r tawelwch	Breaking the stillness
ar draws y rhos	across the moor
larks *a beics*	larks and motor bikes

I'm a pilgrim fallen among tourists. Under umbrellas
along the shore, tucking into lush picnic baskets

Nid llu o saint   No host of saints
yn ymprydio 'ma   fasting here
ar eu gwelyau cerrig on their beds of stone

I say Hi as I pass, but I'm feeling out of it. Suddenly
though I have winged company – a pair of mergansers
soaring and settling.

∾

Second day. I pack my rucksack and leave the guesthouse
before the other visitors come down to breakfast. Last
night I had my fill of questions about 'a woman walking
alone'. 'Is it safe'? 'Are you not afraid?' I wonder about this
as I cross a rolling plateau of unfenced hill farms. What's
to fear on these sheep-bleating, lark-filled heights?

Crist y Bugail   Christ the Shepherd
yn bwydo'r pum mil   feeding the five thousand
oddi ar ei quad bike from his quad bike

Till dusk I follow the banks of the Afon Gam in Nant
yr Eira – the Crooked River in the Valley of Snows. I
sense what Bashō was talking about when he says: 'The
loneliness here's superior to Sumo, the autumn shore.'

Cymuned glòs   Close-knit community
oes 'na bobl sy'n hapus   is there anybody here
gael gair gydag estron?   has a word for a stranger?

ᐤ

Third day. Arrival at Melangell's shrine and Cancer Help Centre, nestling at the head of a green valley. The church stands in a pre-Christian circular enclosure. There is a healing well nearby, but it's been spiked – fenced off by a new owner. I meet friends converging from different directions and we talk too much like you do when you've been alone. Then we sit in the church for an hour, adding our mite to the centuries' silence accumulating there. On the sixteenth-century rood screen Melangell goes on saving a hare from the Prince of Powys's hunting party. All around us are modern carvings of happy hares finding sanctuary under the saint's cloak. *Wyn bach Melangell* – Melangell's lambs, the locals still call hares.

The visitors' book records the testimonies of pilgrims who have come here and have found the help they need to live with their cancer or accept their mortality.

Ar ei hallor   On her shrine
hen gath yn cyrlio   an old cat curling
ac yn canu grwndi   and purring

In the churchyard are the yew trees they say are a thousand years old. Their broken trunks are bleeding red sap, but they still offer shelter to whoever comes, faith or no faith.

Rym ni'n cymryd ein tro We take it in turns
profi tragwyddoldeb   trying on eternity
yn yr ywen gau   in the hollow yew

stone chapel
the bleating of sheep
on a high ridge

Lynne Rees

first warm day
looking for eagles
and finding the sky

Hilary Tann

Short Night on a Bare Mountain

Jane Whittle

It is mid-summer and the moon is full. I am climbing
Cadair Idris to spend the night alone on the summit.
Legend has it that I will return a poet – or mad.

> alone on the mountain
> each slow step draws me closer
> breathing the wind

When I leave the path to rest, I doze in the sun, or in
the shade of stunted Rowan trees beside small waterfalls,
refreshed by their continuous, jaunty movement. Time
relaxes on the longest day.

When I reach the ridge, clouds are beginning to form
over the summit and the air is cold. I climb the rocky
path looking out for a sheltered place to sleep. By
evening all the other climbers have left the mountain,
heading for home. I find a hollow under a huge boulder,
clear away sheep droppings and gather heather for my
bed. At dusk I am arranging the scanty contents of the
rucksack within easy reach of the sleeping bag and its
plastic outer layer – once inside it's not so easy to get
out again – notebook, pencil, torch, water bottle, food,
pills – the old routines seem to require more effort now.

the wind drops
mist creeps over the cliffs
menacing softly

I munch oatcakes and raisins; pour hot Bovril from the thermos carefully into the lid. It tastes wonderful. There is still light in the west but swathes of cloud are pouring across the crags to engulf me. No moon. The silence is huge. I wriggle into my bag, trying to avoid the hardest bits of rock that soon make themselves felt through the heather.

the last stripe of light
slicing the Rhinogs
gutted by night

Perhaps I sleep. Icy water drips into my ear, wind howls through the rocks. The Hounds of Annwn have red ears – they round up the souls of anyone stranded on the mountain and take them away to the *Otherworld*. I snuggle deeper into my bag, tightening the drawstring over my head and dream that the mountain is moving. Raindrops falling on plastic sound like gunshot and wake me. I have slid down the slope, everything is wet. A glimmer of light appears, far away in the east, as a cool breeze begins to shred the enfolding whiteness – wisps and coils of it drag dark tendrils towards me, dissolving before they arrive. Below, newly formed clouds dance with their shadows. I am a part of the sky.

As I crawl from my damp nest, a slope of long grass appears, festooned with bright water drops, swaying like the sea. I turn and stretch my arms to the rising sun. The world at my feet is green and gold. I may not be mad after all, but was that my last ascent?

first up
the lark – invisible
as I am

at the mountain gate black cattle rain-dark slate

Pamela Brown

the cow's measuring eye
dismisses me for more
important things

Robert Drake

dark forest pool
a boy skims his flat stone
across the silence

Caroline Gourlay

A tree falls, someone
you love dies – the same hurt space,
same shudder of light

Tony Curtis

Ar ol y *cull*
mae hi'n gwylio'r gwynt
yn sgubo'r caeau gwag

after the cull
she watches the wind
sweeping the empty fields

Noragh Jones

These hills
have nothing to say
and go on saying it

Ken Jones

Dim mynediad[17] the farmer's sign
The cow parsley
Goes right in

Peter Finch

---

17 No entry

Ghosts of Birchey's Field

Stephen White

Careful footsteps
cast a rare shiver
through a cattle grid's ribs

I remember passing between a horse chestnut and beeches guarding the entrance to Birchey's Field. A blind nag stood, waiting, perhaps hearing my tread on rotten conkers.

A wooden wagon,
frame returning to earth
in a bind of brambles

Hands squeezed into jeans pockets, I followed a dog, bouncing after a ball, fallen near the stones of Ramping Row's remains.

Miners moved out,
moss moved in.
Veils of privet and ash

Past the gorse – its summer stars extinguished – a corrugated stable, scabbed in rust, leaning into the wind. The floor a scatter of cauliflower leaves and squashed hay. I snapped the cricket bat there hitting a six when we were little. Our cries of laughter blew down the breeze like coloured paper.

> In long grass
> a tractor tyre.
> Adders in the summer.

Today, mountain bikers prepare to grimace and glare through mist-sweating hills above. Behind. Buried. Birchey's Field under a fine smear of tar. Their van stands waiting where a horse stood once.

Rippling poplar leaves
a breeze I cannot feel
this autumn

Arwyn Evans

Now

Jane Whittle

Enfolded in spongy grey cloud even grass loses its colour. Grey seeps from water and stone into hills and trees, dissolving their edges, smudging the details of shadow.

Damp rots the bones. I am solid and cold as the land, almost too heavy to breathe.

Low skies cry out for beaten drums to shift them. What songs did they sing to 'make the welkin ring'? They feasted through the night to see how long it would last.

huddled together
blowing sparks from their damp fires
to tickle the stars

One night the cloud clears. The moon – an outsize silver hole in the sky – never had so much black space to travel through. It rises and sets so far north all the shadows go the wrong way.

now
considering a hip operation
I see dewdrops dance

Gwynt o'r gogledd –
o fferm y waun
cyfarth   cyfarth

Wind from the north –
from the moorland farm
barking   barking

Arwyn Evans

All day long
the mist drifts around
the edges of my solitude

Ken Jones

Solitude of the Long Distance Runner

Stephen White

November night at Rhossili, a dry south-westerly storm.
A wooden gate knocks three times on its post and I enter;
descent to the cellar-black shore. Giddy as a sea shanty
I cut through the wind that has come for my bones, to
Burry Holm and back, until I find the steps again. Stagger
up pickled.

> Duel of headlights –
> last bus to Swansea
> is empty

The Scenic Drive at Cwmcarn on a Saturday afternoon.
In the kitchen quiet, I kneel to tie my trainers. Door open,
a breeze brings ice-cream chimes; van in the village – the
dash to queue.

Washing on a line –
white sheets in late May
dry free and easy

*Last year; the London Marathon. I remember … early
morning anticipation sat stony in my throat. Tube train,
famous for ghosts, now bursting with high spirits. The
capital's heart.*

Patter past gingerbread terraces, cigarette-soaked cough
in a doorway sounds like footsteps on wet gravel. Henry

Street is deserted save a red-faced child sitting alone on a curb, slice of white bread in one hand, stick in the other.

> In slips of shadow,
> alley cats' eyes.
> I pad through their turf

A new cafeteria; stone walls and verandas, like a helping of continental après-ski. Behind large tinted panes, sat-back conversation and espressos.

Stench of vinegar, chips;
temptation's last crude assault,
I mouth for the sweet air

. . . the grills, the pubs, the brassy encouragement from Sunday drinkers near Cutty Sark. Sweat on my forehead, grease on the pavements.

The pond like a flat oval of copper-green. Reeded haven for mallards and a lone grebe. A kingfisher zips from a thicket, plunges to mug the silt of a minnow and arcs away, glistening. On a ferny bank, the sound of seeping through young roots. Tongue rough on my palate, I suck the cold air over dry teeth.

> Frosted quarry.
> Silver Birch stands braced
> for fear of shattering

A Jamaican band, steel drums and sunshine. I salute a dreadlocked trumpeter and win a smile. The running river floods Tower Bridge and I peer through cracks in my concentration to marvel at the support – the jubilation.

Purpose and colour
emblazon every runner.
This is for you, Dad

The road meanders amongst evergreens; robed arms usher me through a sacred silence. Weather draws in, the valley floor shrouded. My footsteps fall chalky in the hugging cloud.

Droplets on stubble –
heavy breaths patch easy
to holes in the mist

From Crib y Gwynt – Windy Ridge – a dry-stone wall supports pensioners pointing slowly at Valley Used-to-be. The flannel factory; destroyed in flood. Dr Crow's surgery; houses now.

> Shrill hilltop;
> village in minature.
> The buzzard's realm

The road dips for a flyover. Cars hurtle above, crowd cramped below, samba drums and whistles echo, we surge around the inside bank, gain speed – the race is on.

Final-mile frenzy;
anti-Tamil protest chants,
the sun in my eyes

Isotonic smile ...

Crimson-faced, I return on empty legs to the silent streets, mind glowing on embers of memories. A bat flows like static over a holly bush, spins into the thin evening air. It thieves my attention for a moment.

I listen to owls
unwinding silences
from winter trees

Jane Whittle

Trwy niwl, un cloch –   Through mist, a single bell –
un diferyn ar dy drwyn   a single droplet on your nose

Arwyn Evans

Glaw yng Nghwm Iou.   Rain at Cwm Yoy.
Yr eglwys wag.   The empty church.
Gwrandawaf ar   I listen
sŵn symud hen gerrig   to the swivel of old stones

Arwyn Evans

Shorelines

we do not see
till flight tilts them sunward –
oystercatchers

Nigel Jenkins

sun along the shore
even the grey cockle shells
surprise me

Lynne Rees

last light
footprints running together
into the sea

Jane Whittle

hooter booms –
and a slice of the city
sails into the night

Nigel Jenkins

Ghosts[18]

Arwyn Evans

Come with him tonight, to a fishing-inn along the Wye. To an upstairs room that overlooks the water-meadows and the road. Stand before this open cupboard and . . . just look:

Here is a pair of drooping waders, owned by Mr. Smith. Keep them, he said when he last left. If I don't use them at Three Cocks I won't use them at all. There stands a salmon rod, yellow stained with age. It belonged to Mr. Topjoint. When he stopped visiting, the lady of the house wrote to his last address . . . had no reply.

Here, a mildewed basket and a moth-chewed book of flies. Property of Reverend Snapgut, salmon catcher of renown. Drowned in Australia or some such place. See the tattered net and rusty gaff. The battered hat to fit a sweating brow.

> Shadows in corners.
> The stealth
> in shelving pools.

Tonight there is no fire in the grate. The wind around the chimney mourns and rain beats from the river on the

---

18 Based on an account by A. G. Bradley, in *Highways and Byways in South Wales* (1931).

window glass. But stand with him, and feel the humour of their whiskey and tobacco smoke. Their after-dinner tales. Tonight we are the ghosts.

Trawling between stars
what limpets cling
to spaceship hulls

Arwyn Evans

copper shafts
through bundling grey, beaming up
the Severn Sea

Nigel Jenkins

Sea Songs

Jane Whittle

Bardsey Island floats in the sunset at the end of the Llŷn Peninsula, like a comma at the end of a long phrase – a pause for breath. Wind and tide preclude a landing anywhere along its rocky shores except on the calmest of days, so visitors must prepare to be stranded.

Since the sixth century, people have come here for respite from the world. The Welsh name – Ynys yn y Lli, Island in the Flow – suits it well: water, winds and years flow round this solitary rock. Time seems to stop when you land; it also has less meaning. The bones of Celtic saints are still surfacing from old paths. Thousands of sea birds breed on the cliffs but only a dozen or so people live here all the year round – farmers and fishermen, a few naturalists, sometimes a hermit or a poet. It is a place of legends, sanctity and wild weather. To have arrived is enough.

somewhere to rest
birds of passage feed
on seeds of silence

Alone on the shore all I can hear is the lapping of small waves on the sand. Solfach cove is heaped with brown seaweed smelling of sulphur and salt. The sun is hot, the tide is out. I lean against a warm rock and doze.

                    no wind today
                  someone is humming
                    under the sea

Like Ulysses, beguiled by distant voices strange and new,
I am soon struggling across sharp, slippery rocks towards
them, falling into pools of waving seaweed, grazing my
knees. The water is achingly cold – I should remember
that I am no longer agile enough for such adventures.
The music is muffled by the slapping sounds of water,
but close now just behind the next rock. So I continue
carefully on all fours for a while until, when I look back
. . . the tide has come in and I am much further out than
I thought. With difficulty I return to the beach and do
what I came here to do – sit still and listen.

The songs grow louder-haunting, nostalgic, seductive
notes. Tentatively I try to repeat them.

                    on a rising tide
              voices of the mermaids singing
                    each to each

Hours later, at high tide, wading out waist deep into the
sea, I meet the young ones. Their heads pop up, one by
one, in a semi-circle a few yards away. Wide eyed they
watch, whiskers twitching. Somewhere beyond those
rocks their parents are still singing.

The Irish poet, Sean og Murphy, enticed a female seal inshore by singing a song which pleased her so much she 'fell dead asleep on top of the water'. As the waves rocked her and the tide retreated she was soon left lying on dry land. The next day, I watch this happen in the sheltered bay of Henllwyn. The older seals lie blissfully on their backs, exposing huge pale bellies, waving an occasional lazy flipper, half asleep, rocking in the swell like boats at anchor. When the tide falls, the young ones clamber onto the rocks beside them and the singing begins. I answer, phrase by phrase. As the tide returns the young are shoved off into the water, but their curious puppy faces soon appear again around the rock where I am sitting.

In a collection of Highland Vocal Airs, dated 1784, there is a fisherman's song for attracting *the sea people*, or *selkies*, who were thought to be the spellbound children of the King of Lochlann. Sometimes a fisherman fell in love with a seal woman – beauty, wisdom and bravery were in their blood – and their skins. He would hide her discarded skin so she would stay with him on dry land and bear him children. But, eventually, she would find it again and return to her home under the sea. If the man had been kind to her she might leave gifts of fresh fish on the rocks for her human family.

One seal woman's song, collected by Mrs Kennedy Fraser from the island of Barra, had words too – Ionn da, ionn do, ionn da, odar da hiondan dao, odar da. When she sang this to them the seals replied, 'using the interval of an ascending sixth, a favourite melodic step with the people of the Isles.' Yes, I believe I heard some of those old songs – they are still carried on the wind across Bardsey Island, although the fishermen are not stealing seal skins these days.[19]

no longer alone
while selkies sing with me
I shed an old skin

19   With acknowledgements to David Thomson's *The People of the Sea* and to T. S. Eliot's 'The Lovesong of J. Alfred Prufrock'.

Shingle
in the little swell
a fragile sifting of
our memories

Arwyn Evans

drystone wall
misshapen beach stones rocking
with ancient tides

Marc Evans

Prawns and the Moon

Gillian Drake

On the pavement of a suburban street in Swansea lies a shelled, pink prawn, a fleshy crescent stranded high and dry on a late afternoon in January. No doubt it has fallen out of someone's sandwich: a crustacean without a crust. It probably originated on the other side of the world, where the Indian Ocean beats against the Australian shore and summer is now at its height.

Back home I catch a poem on the Net.

Mandurah prawn boats
Dot with light
The moon-dark river

I gaze out of the window. Here in the northern hemisphere, winter is well advanced. The afternoon deepens into evening, speckling the sky with the cold points of stars.

Born out of itself,
The new moon lies back and stares
At its own shadow

And the computer glows in the navy blue room.

A female river prawn can produce around 2,000 eggs a spawning. The eggs are golden, globular, like little moons. And they change colour, darkening as they grow.

The life of a prawn is dominated by the moon. When young, prawns grow rapidly, moulting their shells to coincide with the full moon (and high tides) each month.

Renewed –
What further use
This cast-off shell

If you hold a shell to your ear, you can hear the sound of the sea. And I hear the same ceaseless impersonal energy in the hum of the computer as it throws onto the screen its catch of facts and figures.

After hatching, young king prawns progress through several larval stages in the ocean and settle in the shallows in coastal bays, or move into the salty lower reaches of estuaries

On the horizon
The bright lights of the harbour
Call travellers home

In late summer, they begin their journey back to the ocean.

It is late evening now. My quest over, I switch off the computer, shut out the beat of the world, and close the curtains against the darkness.

Silence.
My room a sealed shell.
But the tides still pull

e sound of the sea
ɔeaking to my mother
ɔn her birthday

Lynne Rees

I close my book –
a wave breaks its silence
against the rocks

Caroline Gourlay

Black reef ahead
but in the rigging
the song of the wind

Ken Jones

gull hooked, trailing
from its beak a yard of line –
o for a gun

Nigel Jenkins

ar lanw

cylymau   scattered knots of sand
tywod   left by burrowing lugworms
lwgwns   each tide unties them

ar
ddatod

John Rowlands

           one bone-like stone
           unrepeatable
           as the sound of the tide

              Jane Whittle

An Afterword:
Haiku Poetry in Wales

Haiku have been composed in western languages for about a century, but relatively few Welsh writers, in either language, endeavoured much in the form and its relations before the 1990s.

While it is true, as Robert Hass suggests, that 'What is in [haiku] can't be had elsewhere',[20] the haiku – and haiku culture – are by no means as foreign to the Welsh as is sometimes assumed. The parallels between aspects of the early Welsh nature gnome and those of both the haiku and the tanka are almost uncanny. Take, for instance, the thirty-six three-line (occasionally four-line) linked verses of *Englynion Eiry Mynydd* (lit. 'The stanzas of the mountain snow'; twelfth century, author(s) unknown), a selection of which appears in (unrhymed) translation in Tony Conran's *Penguin Book of Welsh Verse* (1967)[21] as

---

20   Robert Hass (ed.), *The Essential Haiku: Versions of Bashō, Buson, and Issa* (Ecco, New York, 1994).
21   Subsequently reissued by Seren Books, in a new edition, as *Welsh Verse* (1986).

'Gnomic Stanzas', and which, as a sequence, is akin to the linked form of Japanese renga. Here are two of them:

> Mountain snow, stag in the ditch;
> Bees are asleep and snug;
> Thieves and a long night suit each other.

> Mountain snow, bare tops of reeds;
> Bent tips of branches, fish in the deep;
> Where there's no learning, cannot be talent.

There are significant differences, of course, between the Welsh and the Japanese forms – the haiku's absence of regular rhyme, for instance – but they have much in common. There's the three-line stanza (although a Japanese haiku traditionally appears as a single vertical line, it is divisible normally into three sections or phrases). There's the strict syllable count (7–7–7 syllables per line in this particular form of *englyn*, the *milwr*; 5–7–5 in a traditional, strict-form haiku). There's the clear seasonal reference – the *kigo* that is a significant characteristic of traditional Japanese haiku – and an almost scientific itemisation of natural phenomena. There are the characteristic attributes of brevity, concision, simplicity, presence, sensory directness and present-tense immediacy. There's a quality of profound attention, often to minutiae, and a sharpness of observation mediated by down-to-earth, unembellished language. While the first two lines of the Welsh tercet perform much like a haiku, the folksy sententiousness of the third line would seem to depart fundamentally from the haiku's disinclination to pass comment. But the aphoristic conclusion drawn at the end of a Welsh gnomic stanza – sometimes rather obvious, but sometimes reminiscent of the oblique wisdom of an oriental koan – shares with many a tanka the moralising inclination of its last two lines. Although the haiku, developing away from the tanka and divesting itself of the older form's tendentious final lines, eschews judgemental generalisations, it is nevertheless profoundly interested, as is the Welsh nature gnome, in the conjunction of the human and the non-human, emphasising the single natural reality that underpins all of existence.

Another parallel between the Welsh and the Japanese literary experience, at least in recent centuries, is an understanding of poetry as an egalitarian and communal activity, in which relatively large numbers of people from all sorts of social backgrounds participate, as both writers and informed readers. If the figure of about one million Japanese writing haiku today (out of a population of 128 million) would seem to give the Japanese a numerical edge over the Welsh in terms of popular engagement in poetry, the packed Eisteddfod pavilion on crowning and chairing days testifies to a broad-based and knowledgeable interest in poetry which is rare in western countries. The *englyn* writer, like the haiku writer, engages with his or her form through a relationship with its past, the essence of which is transmitted by the teachings of an established practitioner and through face-to-face interaction with fellow poets. The notion of an apprenticeship is important in both cultures. What Mark Morris says about the Japanese creative context, in an essay on Buson (1716–84), strikes a notably Welsh chord: 'Shop owner, priest, samurai, actor, wealthy farmer, or petty bureaucrat, the poet was provided with a vantage point on the old poetry and a style growing from it contingent upon his teacher and his *haikai* ancestry. You belonged to all that and it to you ...'[22]

English theorists of the haiku such as R. H. Blyth (1898–1964), casting around for intimations of haiku sensibility in their own literary culture, have often lighted on the Romantic poets, Wordsworth above all, for inadvertent haiku moments, particularly in the poets' meditations upon landscape. With landscape looming so large in Welsh literature, it is no doubt possible to mine pre-modern Welsh poetry for accidental haiku snippets. The poetry of Dafydd ap Gwilym (*fl.* 1320–70), a Romantic (of sorts) centuries before 'The Romantics', might prove fruitful terrain for the haiku prospector. But for conscious and purposeful haiku activity in Wales, we have to look to the second half of the twentieth century – and to endeavours chiefly in the English language. The haiku, so far, has appealed to very few Welsh-language poets, preoccupied as many of them are with the formally more demanding englyn and other daunting structures. If all that most 'mainstream' poets 'know' of the haiku is that it calls for a 5–7–5 syllable count, it's small

---

22   Mark Morris, 'Buson and Shiki: Part One', *Harvard Journal of Asiatic Studies* 44, No.1.

wonder that masters of the intricacies of *cynghanedd*[23] are wont to dismiss the form as being too facile to be worthy of their attention – particularly if even the 5–7–5 'rule' has been abandoned by most contemporary English-language haikuists: all that's left, it must appear, is a smudge of directionless verbiage. There are other characteristics of the haiku that may not appeal to the exponent of (frequently ostentatious) Welsh word-craft: its innate humility; its plain-speaking lack of literary adornment; the almost complete absence of simile and the apparent paucity of metaphor (there *are* metaphors in haiku, but they are usually so undemonstrative as to be barely noticeable); the haiku's avoidance of writerly flamboyance, its downplaying of ego, and its foregrounding of the object and moment of its attention. It is perhaps understandable that this seemingly fugitive form of open-ended minimalism – 'the poetry of emptiness', as it has been described, 'the half-said thing' – should have been slow to make a significant mark in a nation of metaphor junkies, where the exuberant piling on of images, a practice known as *dyfalu*, has been such an admired feature of the *cywyddwr*'s art.[24] But it is disappointing that, to date, relatively few haiku have been written in Welsh, a language whose concrete, grounded

---

23   Literally, 'harmony': an ancient and complex system of sound-chiming within a line of verse, which has been described by the *Princeton Encyclopedia of Poetry and Poetics* (1993) as 'the most sophisticated system of poetic sound-patterning practised in any poetry in the world.'

24   *Cywyddwr*: the maker of a form of poetry known as the *cywydd* which, composed in *cynghanedd*, has lines of seven syllables, arranged in couplets, the accentuation of whose end-rhymes alternates between the lines' final and penultimate syllables.

character – at the opposite end of the spectrum from a more ratiocinatory language such as French – makes it particularly serviceable.

Wales's first serious haiku poet is Tony Conran (1931), who began writing haiku in about 1966 and whose enthusiasm for the form continues undiminished. In 2003, he published *Skimmings*, a collection of fifty-one haiku, and the haiku, 'as a kind of sketch-pad for ideas',[25] informs many of his non-haiku poems. At about the time that he was translating the poems that would appear in *The Penguin Book of Welsh Verse* – including, of course, those haiku-like gnomic stanzas – he was making his first foray into the realm of haiku by writing what should have been a collaborative renga (it appears at the end of the radio ode 'Day Movements' in his *Poems 1951-67*). This, he admits, was not a 'proper' renga because, in the absence of informed collaborators, he wrote the whole thing himself. Like any of the few in Britain at that time who were experimenting with haiku, he was working in complete isolation from others with a similar interest. A post-war enthusiasm in the United States for Japanese culture and religion had sparked a serious engagement with Zen aesthetics among the Beats, chief among them Jack Kerouac, Allen Ginsberg and Gary Snyder, the last two of whom were significant pioneers of the English-language haiku (although it should not be forgotten that an earlier generation had often fallen productively under the haiku's sway: William Carlos Williams and Ezra Pound, for instance; and Wallace Stevens's haiku-

25 Quoted from a letter to Nigel Jenkins from Tony Conran (29/9/2003).

inflected 'Thirteen Ways of Looking at a Blackbird' would in time be echoed by Tony Conran's 'Thirteen Ways of Looking at a Hoover'). Although the haiku news from America was slow to arrive in Britain, there seemed by 1967 to be sufficient interest in the form for the *Guardian* to run a haiku competition: it attracted 3,000 entries, including some, interestingly, in Welsh.

The small-press scene in Britain, with its 'alternative' inclinations and built-in Zen enthusiasms, was considerably more receptive to the haiku (or what purported to be haiku) than most mainstream or 'establishment' outlets. Cardiff's Peter Finch (1947), editor of the eclectic and influential magazine *second aeon* (1966–74), began writing haiku in the late 1960s, in addition to promoting the form in *second aeon* and in the No Walls readings and broadsheets; as a renowned concretist, he would later take the haiku into visual territory.[26] A prominent member of the London small-press scene in the 1960s was Edinburgh-born Chris Torrance (1941) who in 1970 settled in Wales. As both haikuist and (crucially) teacher, Chris Torrance has played a vital and under-acknowledged role in helping to root the haiku in Welsh soil. If much of what passed for haiku in Britain until about 1990 was somewhat off the mark, Chris Torrance won international recognition as a genuine exponent of the art, publishing 'Seven Winter Haiku' in Mike Horovitz's famous Penguin anthology *Children of Albion: Poetry of the Underground in Britain* (1969) and being hailed in America, in William J Higginson's landmark

---

26   See his collection *The Welsh Poems* (Shearsman, 2006).

'how to' guide, *The Haiku Handbook* (1985), as one of the four most significant haiku poets of Britain. His pioneering extra-mural creative writing classes at the University of Wales, Cardiff (now Cardiff University) introduced scores of venturesome new writers to the haiku and its related forms.

The 1970 to 1990 period in Wales, as in Britain generally, seemed to generate little haiku activity, with mainstream poets tending to dismiss the haiku as some faddy hangover from the 1960s – if, indeed, they paid it any regard at all. But quietly, haphazardly, some sort of foundation was being laid. Tony Conran in the north was persevering with his one-man renga-making (see, for example, 'Ten Morning Songs' in *Spirit Level*, Gomer, 1974) and experimenting with tanka ('Six Poems about God', in the same volume). Peter Finch and Chris Torrance in Cardiff, and Phil Maillard (1948) and Nigel Jenkins (1949) in Swansea were offering the haiku as an essential component of writing courses for organisations such as the Welsh Academy, the WEA and university extra-mural departments, and there was occasional contact with established haikuists from further afield. Bill Wyatt (1942), for instance, another 'Child of Albion' and one of the few English haiku writers at that time to have been noted in America, gave a memorable reading in the early 1980s – of nothing but haiku – to a capacity audience in Swansea's Singleton Hotel.

Since about 1990, the haiku pace has perceptibly quickened. The founding in that year of the British Haiku Society – by the English haikuists David Cobb (1926) and Dee Evetts (1943) – gave haiku enthusiasts their first opportunity to meet each other, and to debate, publish and promote a literary form whose development in the countries of Britain had been impeded by the isolation of its practitioners and by the lack of consensus as to what, in British and European terms (rather than according to the dominant American ethos), might constitute a functioning haiku on this side of the Atlantic. Respecting the integrity of the nations and regions of Britain, the BHS has sought to foster not 'the British haiku' (perish the grotesque thought) but a theory and practice appropriate to the making of haiku wherever in these islands poets find themselves working. Although some sort of definitional consensus – which pays proper regard to Japanese essentials while acknowledging the need to adapt the form to indigenous conditions – seems by now to have been reached, vigorous debate continues on many related issues, with national and regional branches flying the flag for local particularity and diversity. Perhaps only half of Britain's haiku writers belong to the BHS, but all have benefited from its educational and promotional work and from the articulate advocacy of local representatives in Wales who have sought to understand and develop the haiku in Welsh cultural terms.

The first event of national significance in the development of the haiku in Wales was the Welsh Academy's 1991 Japan Festival Haiku Competition, which was the first major international haiku contest to be organised in any of the countries of Britain for twenty-four years. It attracted over a thousand entries in English from all over the world, although only three of the Welsh entries – one by Marc Evans (1957) of Cardiff, and two by John Rowlands (1947) then of Cardiff – made it through to the 'highly commended' category. Part of the prize was publication in the *New Welsh Review*.[27] With the exception of *second aeon*, the *NWR* was therefore probably the first Welsh magazine ever to pay the haiku serious attention.

The winner of that competition was David Cobb who by then was well on his way to becoming one of the most accomplished haikuists in the English-speaking world.[28] He has maintained contact with the developing haiku scene in Wales ever since, visiting Swansea to take part in various haiku events at the Dylan Thomas Centre and Swansea University. On one such occasion, five of Wales's haiku poets – Ken Jones (1930), Noragh Jones (1936) Peter Finch, Arwyn Evans (1940) and Nigel Jenkins combined with musicians Peter Stacey and Dylan Fowler to present an innovatory programme of haiku backed by minimalist improvisations on flute and guitar.

A more significant innovation in Wales (as in England) since about the late 1990s has been the haibun. While David Cobb, initially, led the way in England, the pioneers in Wales have been Ken Jones, Noragh Jones and Matt Morden (1962). The publication in 2001 by Ken Jones's Pilgrim Press of a three-man[29] haiku and haibun anthology, *Pilgrim Foxes*, was a milestone.

---

27 The *New Welsh Review* No. 15 (Vol. IV, No. 3; Winter 1991–92).
28 For a profile of David Cobb, see Nigel Jenkins's essay 'Batting for Essex, England – and the World' in *Planet* 173, October/November 2005.
29 The three *Pilgrim Foxes* are Ken Jones and two Irish poets, James Norton and Seán O'Connor.

As well as publishing haiku and haibun, Ken Jones has also been concerned to disseminate his thoughts on the theory of these forms, particularly as there is not yet the consensus about the nature of the haibun as there is about that of the haiku. Another significant Welsh theorist of the haiku is Tony Conran, most of whose invaluable insights on this subject have been confined so far to personal communication in letter form. His elucidation of the three classical attributes of the haiku is worth quoting at length:

> The haiku is a sociable but not a social form. It is almost totally unrhetorical, having nothing to say to the will. It does not have an agenda of social change, except possibly to persuade other people to write haiku in reply. From all this flow the three classical haiku attributes – loneliness, tenderness and slenderness. A haiku represents a sharing of a moment in a great loneliness; what is shared is centred on the feeling of loneliness itself, however much other feelings are involved with it. Loneliness is the gift the haiku poet prizes above all, because it is the loneliness of detachment, not the bitter isolation of frustrated desire. Within that detachment one's feelings can grow, not as the ravishers of virtue they normally are, but as Christ says God feels compassion for the fall of a sparrow. Haiku poets like Bashō call it tenderness – fellow-feeling, a gentle acknowledgement that things exist outside yourself, which suffer and have their being in the Tao of enlightenment just as you do. And a haiku must be

slender because it makes no claims upon you other than an invitation to share its moment.[30]

Tony Conran acknowledges the importance of a shared understanding of what the haiku is about; he has also stressed awareness of its civilizational implications. Some informal renga experiments with friends might have got somewhere had there been poets to call upon who knew what they were doing:

> If all the poets of Wales could be given prison-sentences – say, six months – and told they had to split into groups of five and each group to produce at least 20 haiku a day, gradually increasing to 100, we might find ourselves in a tradition where haiku-writing was the norm, and, more important, had standards and a literary aesthetic of its own.

Since the mid 1990s, the universities have played an increasingly significant role in establishing a haiku aesthetic. In 2001, Martin Lucas (1959), studying at Cardiff, completed his groundbreaking PhD thesis, *Haiku in Britain, Theory, Practice, Context*, and the creative writing faculties of most of Wales's higher education establishments have at least one member of staff who is experienced in and enthusiastic about the haiku. (On the other hand, unlike in England, there is no statutory obligation to teach the haiku in Welsh schools; although teachers are free to introduce the form if they wish, one suspects that in most cases consideration of the haiku advances little beyond the counting of syllables.)

30   Quoted from Tony Conran's letter to Nigel Jenkins, 29/9/2003.

The increasing strength of the haiku in Wales was recognised by the Welsh Haiku Millennium Project, initiated by Ken Jones and Arwyn Evans. As a result of invitations being sent to 23 known haiku enthusiasts in Wales, a selection of 14 haiku from Wales formed the Welsh contribution to a celebration of haiku in the four countries of Britain entitled *The Omnibus Anthology of Haiku and Senryu*,[31] edited by Fred Schofield (Hub Editions, 2001). Six years later, in 2007, the editor of *Planet: The Welsh Internationalist* invited Nigel Jenkins, Ken Jones and Lynne Rees (1958) to engage in a discussion about haiku, in the magazine's series of email debates, 'Exchanges'.

As the debate broadens and matures, and as more haiku and haibun are published in Wales, there are encouraging signs that a haiku aesthetic pertinent to Welsh cultural conditions is beginning to be articulated (although it has to be said that by no means all of Wales's haiku writers conceive of themselves as operating in a Welsh literary context). As elsewhere, the haiku has its dedicated specialists who tend to devote most of their energies to that form and its relations, chief among them Ken Jones (whose haiku are informed by, and a function of, his Zen Buddhism), Noragh Jones, Matt Morden, Arwyn Evans, Jane Whittle (1931), Pamela Brown (1946) and Caroline Gourlay (1939). But there are increasing numbers of 'mainstream' poets, in or of Wales, for whom the haiku constitutes an important part

---

31   Senryu: a form of haiku which tends to foreground humour, having a greater interest in human relations and inclined towards the satirical.

of their poetic endeavour, among them Tony Conran, Chris Torrance, Peter Finch, Philip Gross (1952), Lynne Rees and Humberto Gatica (1944). The perceived divide between these two 'communities' – with the specialists sometimes complaining that too many mainstream poets' haiku are distractingly 'literary', if not verging on 'poesy', and the mainstream establishment declining to recognise the specialists as 'serious' (and publishable, therefore, in mainstream outlets) – has tended to retard the haiku's development (on both sides of the Dyke). So too has the fact that until recently few of Wales's serious haiku practitioners have been under fifty years of age. During the early years of the present century, however, several promising young poets with a more occasional but nevertheless knowledgeable commitment to the form have begun to emerge from the growing number of creative writing classes. The haiku in Wales seems at last to be spreading its wings.

NIGEL JENKINS

BIOGRAPHICAL NOTES

RICK ALLDEN, born in Coventry in 1981, moved to Wales in 2001 and studied at Swansea University, graduating with a Masters in creative and media writing in 2006. He lives with his partner in Ystrad Mynach in the Rhymney Valley, and is a freelance writer and producer of plays and comedy sketches. In 2009, he co-founded Inky Quill Productions.

PAMELA BROWN was born in Lancashire in 1946. She worked as a secretary in Manchester for five years, before moving to the High Peak District where she worked mainly with horses. In 1980, she came to Wales to work as a shepherd, and then in 1990 bought a derelict farm in the parish of Llanbrynmair where she developed her own breeding flock. Retired, she lives temporarily in Carno. She has published in *Acorn*, *Blithe Spirit*, *Presence*, the *Red Moon Anthology* and Snapshot Press's *Haiku Calendar*. In 2009, she won the Haiku Presence Award.

MARION CARLISLE was born in 1958 into a musical family near London, and studied classical piano and later political science in Leeds. Having spent many childhood holidays on a farm near Llangranog, Ceredigion, in 2002 she settled in north Pembrokeshire. She is a musician, voice therapist and poet, inspired, as both poet and composer, by the landscape of west Wales. Her piano solo CD *Open the Sky* was released on the Fflach label in 2004.

SARAH COLES, born in Swansea in 1971, writes poetry, fiction, reviews and features. She has published work in various online magazines, and takes part in spoken-word events across south Wales. She has a Master's degree in creative writing from Swansea University, and teaches creative writing in Swansea's Department of Adult and Continuing Education. She lives in Dunvant, Swansea, with her three daughters.

TONY CONRAN, Wales's first serious haiku practitioner, was born in India in 1931, but has lived mostly in north Wales, where he was a tutor in English at Bangor University. He is well known as a poet, translator and critic, with over 20 published books. His translations include *The Penguin Book of Welsh Verse* (1967), subsequently reissued as *Welsh Verse* (Seren Books). His poetry publications include *Blodeuwedd* (Seren Books, 1989), *Castles* (Gomer, 1993), *Red Sap of Love* (Gwasg Carreg Gwalch, 2006) and *What Brings You Here So Late* (Gwasg Carreg Gwalch, 2008).

TONY CURTIS, born in Carmarthen in 1946, is Professor of Poetry at the University of Glamorgan, where he founded the M.Phil in Writing. He has written haiku occasionally through his career: one of the poems selected here come from a sequence in response to the photographs of Fred Jones (of Llanymynach and Illinois). His ninth collection was *Crossing Over* (Seren, 2007). He recently completed *Real South Pembrokeshire* for Seren's Real Wales series and has edited *The Meaning of Apricot Sponge* – the selected writings of John Tripp (Parthian, 2010).

GILLIAN DRAKE was born in Barry in 1958 and now lives in Swansea with her husband Robert. Her two children's books were both published by Pont; other published work includes short stories, articles and poems in various outlets.

She graduated from UCW Aberystwyth in 1979, and gained an MA in creative writing from Swansea University in 2005. She has worked in the voluntary sector, in areas as diverse as archaeology, mental health and educational publishing.

ROBERT DRAKE, born in Leigh, Lancashire in 1956, settled in Wales some thirty years ago. Following a doctorate in disability policy (1992) he became senior lecturer in social policy at Swansea University and subsequently taught political theory at the Open University. He first wrote haiku at school under the guiding hand of teacher and poet John Cassidy. A first collection of haiku, *In Fading Light*, is in preparation. He lives in Swansea with his partner, Gillian.

ARWYN EVANS, who lives in Crumlin, Gwent, was born (1940) and bred in the Rhymney Valley. After a year at Coleg Harlech, he graduated from Bangor University in 1970 and lectured for ten years at Warley College in the English west Midlands. Subsequently a tutor and manager at adult education colleges in his home area, he retired in 2005. It was *The Penguin Book of Japanese Verse* which introduced him to haiku in the mid 1960s, since when he has published in many of the main haiku outlets. His collection *The Cold Between My Toes* was produced in a limited edition by Stonebridge Publications in 2007, to coincide with his first photographic exhibition.

MARC EVANS, born in Cardiff in 1957 and raised a monoglot in Fflint, came home to the capital after graduating in Welsh at Aberystwyth in 1980. His first poem in *Poetry Wales* (aged 16) was his last for decades, as he had divorced his mother tongue for a new language. He worked in broadcasting, with BBC Radio Cymru and HTV, and currently works in the fields of public relations and public affairs. His haiku have appeared in *Blithe Spirit* (the journal of the British Haiku

Society) and *Poetry Wales*.

PETER FINCH was born in 1947 in Cardiff, where he still lives. He is chief executive of Academi, the Welsh National Literature Promotion Agency and Society for Writers. His books include *Antibodies* (Stride, 1997), *The Welsh Poems* (Shearsman, 2006), together with *Food* (2001), *Useful* (1997), *Selected Later Poems* (2007), and *Zen Cymru* (2010), all published by Seren. He is the creator and editor of the *Real* series of psychogeographies published by Seren. His own titles include *Real Cardiff One* (2002), *Two* (2004) and *Three* (2009) and *Real Wales* (2008). www.peterfinch.co.uk

HUMBERTO GATICA, born in 1944, is a Chilean poet and photographer living in Swansea, where he and his family sought political asylum following the 1973 military coup. He writes chiefly in Spanish, and published a bilingual collection, *The Sand Garden*, in 2008 (Hafan Books). But, he says, 'The experience of the haiku moment comes to me in English and it is in English that I write the first draft. Sometimes I translate it and work a version in Spanish.' He works in the Dynevor Centre for Art, Design and Media at Swansea Metropolitan University.

EIRWYN GEORGE, born in 1936 in Tufton, Pembrokeshire, lives in Maenclochog. After graduating at Aberystwyth, he taught Welsh and history in schools in Narberth and Crymych, and then worked for the county library service at Haverfordwest for fifteen years before retiring. A distinguished local historian and poet, he won the Crown at the National Eisteddfod in 1982 and 1993, and in 2001 he won the National Eisteddfod's first (and so far only) prize for a collection of haiku. His latest publication is an autobiography, *Fel Hyn y Bu* (Lolfa, 2010).

CAROLINE GOURLAY, born in London in 1939 and raised in Shropshire, has lived all her married life in Knighton, Powys. She became involved in the British Haiku Society in 1994 and edited their journal *Blithe Spirit* from 1998 to 2000. Her collections include *Crossing the Field* (Redlake Press, 1995), *Reading All Night* (Hub Press, 1999), *Through the Café Door* (Snapshot Press, 2000) and *Lull Before Dark* (Brooks Books, USA, 2005). In 1996, she won the James Hackett International Haiku Award. Fifty of her tanka appeared in the *Poetry Monthly* anthology *This Country* (2005).

PHILIP GROSS was born in north Cornwall, beside Delabole slate quarry, in 1952. In 2004, he crossed the water from Bristol to become Professor of Creative Writing at the University of Glamorgan, and now lives with his wife Zélie in Penarth. He is the author of novels, plays and some fifteen collections of poetry, for adults and young people. *The Water Table* (Bloodaxe, 2009) won the 2009 T.S. Eliot Prize and *I Spy Pinhole Eye* (Cinnamon, 2009) the 2010 Wales Book of the Year prize.

KAREN HOY was born in Newport in 1966, and lived in Caldicot, Caerphilly and Cwmbran before moving to Hertfordshire. Her work has appeared in such outlets as Snapshot Press's *Haiku Calendar*, *Presence* magazine and the British Haiku Society's journal *Blithe Spirit*. Karen has worked on documentaries and wildlife films for the BBC, *National Geographic*, the Discovery Channel and other leading broadcasters. In 2006, she founded the TV development company Gilded Lily.

JOAN E. JAMES, who lives in Cardiff with her husband Gwyn Ingli James, was born in Llantwit Major in 1929. A teacher-training course at Bishop Otter College, Chichester was followed by a year teaching at the École Normale d'Institutrices in Poitiers. A pioneer of the teaching of French in secondary modern schools in the 1950s, she returned to live in Wales in 1969. She has written stories, articles and poems, although rarely for publication; some of her haiku, however, have appeared in *Blithe Spirit* and *Presence*.

NIGEL JENKINS, born in 1949, teaches creative writing at Swansea University. His books include two haiku collections, *Blue* and *O For a Gun* (Planet Books, 2002 and 2007). His latest publications are *Real Swansea* (Seren, 2008) and, with the artist David Pearl, *Gower* (Gomer Press, 2009), a celebration in prose, poetry and photography of his native Gower. Winner of the Wales Book of the Year prize in 1996 for his travel book *Gwalia in Khasia* (Gomer Press, 1995), he is co-editor of *The Welsh Academy Encyclopaedia of Wales* (University of Wales Press, 2008).

KEN JONES, who lives in Cwmrheidol, near Aberystwyth, with his Irish wife Noragh, was born in 1930. He is a Zen practitioner and teacher, and author of books on socially engaged Buddhism. Co-editor of the quarterly *Contemporary Haibun Online*, his collections include *Arrow of Stones* (British Haiku Society, 2002), *Stallion's Crag* (Iron Press, 2003), *The Parsley Bed* (Pilgrim Press, 2006) and *Stone Leeks* (Pilgrim Press 2009).

NORAGH JONES was born in 1936 in Northern Ireland, and worked in Trinity College Dublin Library before leaving Ireland. In 1980, she and her husband Ken Jones settled in an old farmhouse in Cwmrheidol, near Aberystwyth. She has taught in adult education and learnt Welsh. Her books include the haiku and haiku-prose collection *Stone Circles* (Pilgrim Press, 2004); it contains the haibun sequence 'Songs of Old Age', which won the Noboyuki Yuasa International Haibun Contest in 2003.

ALAN KELLERMANN, born in Wisconsin (USA) in 1979, works at the Dylan Thomas Centre in Swansea and is studying for a creative writing PhD at Swansea University, having earlier taken his Masters in creative writing there. He is a member of the editorial board of the *Swansea Review*. His poetry has appeared in journals such as *Planet, Agenda, Poetry Ireland Review*, and in the anthology *Nu: Fiction and Stuff* (Parthian, 2009). In 2009, he published a poetry chapbook, *Something God Doesn't Know*.

VIV KELLY, born in 1963, settled in Wales in 2002, after a sojourn on Achill Island off the Atlantic coast of Ireland. She was among the first cohort of students to complete the MA in creative and media writing at Swansea University where, she says, she gained a new appreciation of the art of haiku and haibun. Her work is inspired by the landscapes of Wales and Ireland. A counsellor, shamanic practitioner and trainer, she lives in Brynamman, Carmarthenshire.

RONA LAYCOCK was born in Bangor, Gwynedd, in 1951 but has lived and travelled in many countries. She runs creative-writing workshops in and around Gloucestershire, where she now lives, and her work has been published in various magazines and anthologies. Haiku and haibun formed a significant part of her PhD project at Swansea University, where she studied (initially for a creative writing MA) between 2005 and 2010. Editor of the writing magazine *Graffiti*, her first poetry collection, *Borderlands*, was published as an audio CD in 2009.

LESLIE MCMURTRY, who was born in Albuquerque, New Mexico, in 1984, has an MA in creative writing from Swansea University. She has spent most of the last decade living in Swansea, where she worked for a while at the Dylan Thomas Centre. Leslie has published poetry in *Lunarosity, Borderlines,*

Decanto and *Poetry Wales*. She is pursuing a PhD at Swansea on radio drama in Europe and the US (where her play *The Mesmerist* was broadcast on Public Radio in 2010).

MATT MORDEN was born in Usk, Monmouthshire, in 1962. He has lived in Carmarthenshire since 1992 (shortly before he began writing haiku and senryu) and works as a local government officer. His work features in the leading haiku outlets, and Snapshot Press have published two collections of his work, *A Dark Afternoon* (2002) and *Stumbles in Clover* (2007); his writing now appears regularly at www.mordenhaikupoetry.blogspot.com.

JAYNE RAFFERTY was born in Rotherham in 1982 and moved to Wales in 2000 to study at Swansea University, graduating in 2006 with a Masters in creative and media writing. She lives with her partner in Uplands, Swansea and works as an English teacher in a secondary school.

LYNNE REES was born in 1958 in the house where her parents still live, on Sandfields Estate, Port Talbot. In 1978, she relocated to Jersey to work in offshore banking and moved to Kent in 1985, where she ran her own second-hand and antiquarian bookshop for twelve years. She is a graduate of the Masters programme at the University of Glamorgan, a poet, novelist, award-winning creative writing tutor, and editor. In 2009, she co-edited the BHS biennial Haibun Anthology, *An Unseen Wind*, and is an adjudicator for the new British Haiku Awards launched in 2010. www.lynnerees.com

JOHN ROWLANDS, who lives and paints in Tremadog, Gwynedd, was born in Llanrhystud, Ceredigion, in 1947. Widely exhibited, he studied art in Cardiff, Bristol and Trinity College, Carmarthen, worked as an art teacher in Buxton, Ystradgynlais and Aberystwyth, and was for some years art education officer at the National Museum in Cardiff. Winner of the crown in the Pontrhydfendigaid Eisteddfod in 1986, he has published two books with Y Lolfa, *Aber* (1986, in Y Lolfa's *Beirdd Answyddogol* series) and *Annwyl Arholwr* (1990).

JON SUMMERS was born in Pontypool in 1969, and grew up in Newbridge, Gwent. He graduated from Swansea University in 1990, and now lives and works in south-east Wales as an IT consultant. His work has been published in *Blithe Spirit*, *Presence*, *Taboo Haiku*, *Borderlines* and *Tinywords*, among others. He edited and published the small-press poetry magazines *Ah Pook Is Here* and *Barfly* during the 1990s, and now finds his time increasingly occupied with a growing family.

HILARY TANN, an internationally renowned composer, was born in 1947 in Ferndale, Rhondda, where she spent her childhood and which nurtured the love of nature which has inspired all her music. She holds degrees in composition from the University of Wales at Cardiff and from Princeton University. Hilary lives in the foothills of the Adirondack Mountains in Upstate NY where she is Professor of Music at Union College. She is a founding member of the Route 9 Haiku Group which publishes the biannual anthology *Upstate Dim Sum* (www.upstatedimsum.com).

VICKY THOMAS was born in Caerphilly in 1982, where she still lives. After graduating in English from the University of Glamorgan, she studied for an MA in creative writing at Swansea University, completing in 2005. She has worked since then as a teacher.

STEPHEN TOFT was born in 1980 in Hampshire but grew up in Mumbles, Swansea. He currently lives in Lancashire where he works with young adults with autism and learning difficulties. His poetry has been published in various journals and anthologies, among them *Blithe Spirit*, *Frogpond*, *Presence* and *Snapshots*. In 2008, the American haiku press Red Moon published his first collection, *the kissing bridge*.

CHRIS TORRANCE was born in Edinburgh in 1941 and grew up in the London area. He became an editor of the mid-1960s small magazine *Origins Diversions*, when he started writing seriously, being one of the first recognised haiku practitioners in Britain. Chris moved to an old farmhouse near Glynneath, in the Neath Valley, in 1970, where he began his long poem-series *The Magic Door*. He spent 25 years as a creative-writing tutor for the University of Wales, Cardiff, and founded the poetry and music band Poetheat (now Heatpoets) with Chris Vine in 1986.

MARY B. VALENCIA was born in 1973 to francophone parents in St. Eustache, Québec and grew up living in Québec, France, England and Ontario; she lives in Toronto. Mary pursued a Masters in creative writing at Swansea University (2006–7) precisely because of Wales's rich bilingual culture. Her writing has appeared in publications such as the *New Welsh Review*, *Descant* and *PRISM International*. She is currently completing a collection of Wales-inspired short stories, *One Block from the Prison, Two Blocks from the Sea*.

BRIAN WHITE was born in Birmingham in 1938, and worked as an accountant. He moved to Swansea in 1983 and, after retirement, took a degree in English at Swansea University, which he followed up with an MA in creative writing at Trinity College, Carmarthen. He has published poetry and short stories in various magazines, and haiku and tanka in *Presence* and *Blithe Spirit*.

STEPHEN WHITE was born in 1982 in Newport, Monmouthshire, and grew up in the nearby village of Cwmcarn. He holds a degree in French and Italian with European Studies from the University of Bath and qualified as an English-language teacher in 2007. He has since taught English in Paris, Bari (southern Italy) and Cardiff. Currently completing a creative writing MA at Swansea University, he lives in Penclawdd, north Gower, and works as a lifeguard at the leisure centre in Swansea.

JANE WHITTLE, who settled in Dyffryn Dysynni, Gwynedd, in 1989, after a lifetime as a visitor, was born in Cambridge in 1931. She is an artist and writer whose work is mostly about places and journeys. In the 1970s and 1980s, she published numerous illustrated articles and a book, and her poetry occasionally appeared in magazines and anthologies. In 1995, she began to write haiku and haibun, which have since appeared in outlets such as *Blithe Spirit*, *Snapshots*, *Presence*, *Modern Haiku*, the Redthread website, and British and American anthologies.

JAN WIGLEY, who was born in Birmingham in 1961, spent the first six years of her life in Baghdad, Iraq, and settled in Wales in 1985; she lives at Llangennith in west Gower with her partner Si and their five children. She is a counsellor and play-therapist, working mainly with children and their families, 'unravelling the knots in their stories'. In 2008, she completed Swansea University's MA in creative writing.

ELOISE WILLIAMS was born in Cardiff in 1972, and lives in Llantrisant. She has worked in theatre and drama since 2000, and currently teaches adults with learning disabilities. Eloise has published poetry and short stories in various publications, including Honno's anthology *Cut on the Bias* (2010), and has won several awards in literary competitions.

She is currently studying for an MA in creative writing at Swansea University.

RHYS OWAIN WILLIAMS was born in 1987 and raised in Swansea. Having completed an English with creative writing degree at Swansea University, he continued to study there for an MA in creative writing(2009–10). He has published in various magazines, including the online broadsheet that accompanied *Agenda*'s Welsh Issue in 2008. Rhys is a regular reader at spoken-word events across south Wales.

ACKNOWLEDGEMENTS

It was Stephen Toft, when he was living in Mumbles, who first proposed an anthology of haiku poetry from Wales. We are grateful to him for starting the ball rolling, and to Arwyn Evans who then picked it up and ran with it, before passing it on to the present editorial team. We have benefited considerably from Stephen's and Arwyn's groundwork, and from help and advice from others, among them John Barlow and Jim Kacian. We would like to thank all the poets who contributed to this book.[32] The project was administered from Swansea University: Nigel Jenkins in particular is grateful, as ever, to colleagues in the university's Department of English Language and Literature for their interest and support.

Acknowledgements are due to the publishers and organisers of the following, where some of these poems first appeared: *Acorn, American Tanka, big sky* (Red Moon Press, 2007), *Blithe Spirit* (Journal of the British Haiku Society), *Blue* by Nigel Jenkins (Planet Books, 2002), *Common Source* (The Anglo-Welsh Poetry Society's Members' Anthology), *Contemporary Haibun Online, Contemporary Haibun 10* (Red Moon Press, 2008), *Dover Beach and My Back Yard* (BHS Haibun Anthology, 2009), *dust of summers* (Red Moon Press, 2008), *Hermits* and

---

32   The inclusion in an anthology of work by its editor(s) has sometimes proved controversial. The three editors of this anthology submitted work for consideration in the same way as other contributors, and the final selection, in each case, was made by the other two editors.

Hermit Particles by Barry Edgar Pilcher, Chris Torrance and Bill Wyatt (Canna Press, 2003 and forthcoming, respectively), *Haibun Today*, *Frogpond* (Journal of the Haiku Society of America), the annual *Haiku Calendar* published by Snapshot Press, *Haiku Presence*, *Haiku Quarterly*, *Haiku Spirit*, *Hidden* (BHS Members' Anthology, 2008), *Journeys to Wales 2003–2006* by Fred Jones and with Tony Curtis, *Lull Before Dark* by Caroline Gourlay (Brooks Books, 2005), *Modern Haiku*, *Notes to the Gean* (Gean Tree Press), *O For a Gun* by Nigel Jenkins (Planet Books, 2007), *Orbis*, *Planet: The Welsh Internationalist*, *Presence*, the R. H. Blyth Award, *Reading All Night* by Caroline Gourlay (Hub Press, 1999), *Roundyhouse*, *Sea* (BHS Members' Anthology, 2006), *Shamrock*, *Simply Haiku*, *Skimmings* by Tony Conran (Deiniol Press,2003), *Snapshots*, *Taken for Pearls* by Tony Curtis (Seren, 2003), *The Heron's Nest*, *This Country / Poetry Monthly*, *Through the Café Door* by Caroline Gourlay (Snapshot Press, 2000), the *Upstate Dim Sum* (biannual anthology of the Route 9 Haiku Group), *white lies* (Red Moon Press, 2009), *Wing Beats: British Birds in Haiku*, edited by John Barlow and Matthew Paul (Snapshot Press, 2008) and the With Words International Haiku Competition.

INDEX OF AUTHORS